# Diving & Snorkeling

# Palau

D1563848

Tim Rock

Francis Toribiong

LONELY PLANET PUBLICATIONS
Melbourne • Oakland • London • Paris

Diving & Snorkeling Palau
- A Lonely Planet Pisces Book

2nd Edition – September, 2000
1st Edition – 1994, Gulf Publishing Company

Published by
Lonely Planet Publications
192 Burwood Road, Hawthorn, Victoria 3122, Australia

Other offices
150 Linden Street, Oakland, California 94607, USA
10A Spring Place, London NW5 3BH, UK
1 rue du Dahomey, 75011 Paris, France

Photographs
by Tim Rock (unless otherwise noted)

Front cover photograph
Partially closed pink sea anemone
by Tim Rock

Back cover photographs, by Tim Rock
The colorful and unique mandarinfish
Yellow coral polyps bloom at Yellow Wall
Aerial view of Long Lake in the Rock Islands

The images in this guide are available for licensing
from Lonely Planet Images
email: lpi@lonelyplanet.com.au

ISBN 1 86450 019 0

text & maps © Lonely Planet 2000
photographs © photographers as indicated 2000
dive site maps are Transverse Mercator projection

LONELY PLANET and the Lonely Planet logo are
trademarks of Lonely Planet Publications Pty Ltd.

Printed by H&Y Printing Ltd., Hong Kong

# Contents

# Authors

## Tim Rock

Tim Rock attended the journalism program at the University of Nebraska, Omaha and has been a professional broadcast and print photojournalist for 25 years. The majority of those years have been spent in the Western and Indo Pacific reporting on environmental and conservation issues. His television series *Aquaquest Micronesia* was an Ace Award finalist. He has also produced six documentaries on the history and undersea fauna of the region. He has won the prestigious Excellence in the Use of Photography from the Society of Publishers in Asia. He also lists many other awards for photography and writing, publishes a magazine and works as a correspondent for numerous Pacific Rim magazines. He is the author or co-author of four other Lonely Planet Pisces books including *Chuuk Lagoon, Pohnpei & Kosrae, Bali, Guam & Yap* and *Papua New Guinea*. Rock lives on Guam with his wife Larie.

Tim Rock's photographic equipment is varied and includes Nikonos II, III, IV & V cameras, Housed Nikons in Aquatica housings and Nikonos RSAF cameras and lenses. His strobes are made by Nikon and Ikelite. Land cameras are the F5, F100 and N90 by Nikon and Nikkor lenses.

## Francis Toribiong

Francis Toribiong attended Long Beach State University majoring in Anthropology. While in college, he learned to scuba dive, became an instructor, and learned to sky dive. He worked in college as a member of the lifeguard team in Laguna Beach. He used his skills to pioneer adventure tourism in Palau. That effort blossomed into Fish N' Fins Palau, established in January of 1979. It is one of the longest operating diving companies in Koror. Toribiong and his crew are responsible for finding most of the major dive sites now so popular in Palau. He also teamed up with Klaus Lindemann to discover most of Palau WWII shipwrecks and the book *Desecrate One* is the result of that work. He was also recently featured in the IMAX Emmy winner, *The Living Sea*. Toribiong sold his diving and hotel interests in Palau and now he and his wife Susan live with their five children in the U.S. Pacific Northwest.

## From the Author, *by Tim Rock*

For nearly two decades I have been truly blessed to be diving the Palau Islands. The reefs, walls, channels and wrecks are unrivaled in the world. The saying "Palau has it all" couldn't be truer. By sharing my experiences and photos, I hope to encourage divers worldwide to help protect these most marvelous marine resources. I have logged hundreds of dives with Francis Toribiong, my dive buddy and co-author. His spirit of exploration and adventure is the reason many of these incredible underwater discoveries have been found. He has always led an unselfish crusade to preserve and protect the rich natural and cultural resources of his homeland for the benefit of visitors, local education and future generations. I wholly support his and his wife Susan's goals as we proudly present this co-authored guide for the enjoyment of visiting divers worldwide. Through this book, we hope to promote these marvelous dive destinations so Palauans may share with the world their culture and environment.

I would also like to thank longtime friends Sam and Felicia Scott who have also been leaders in the Palau dive industry. They have provided me with moral and logistical support, superb site information and—especially—lots of laughs over the years.

## From the Publisher

This second edition was produced in Lonely Planet's U.S. office under the help and expertise of publishing manager Roslyn Bullas. Senior editor Debra Miller edited the text and photos, with valuable assistance from Roslyn. Emily Douglas designed the book and cover, and kept the buoy afloat during production. Thanks to Sarah J.H. Hubbard for early editing help and to Tullan Spitz for donning her proofreader's mask. Cartographer Patrick Bock created the maps with his usual enthusiasm, attention and flare. Excellent map help also came from Sara Nelson, John Spelman and U.S. cartography manager Alex Guilbert. Portions of the text were adapted from Lonely Planet's *South Pacific* and *Micronesia*. Lindsay Brown reviewed the marine life section for scientific accuracy. Special thanks to Tim Rock for his overwhelming passion for Palau, for his stunning photographs that capture its alluring, delicate resources, and for his infinite humor from across the sea.

## Lonely Planet Pisces Books

Lonely Planet acquired the Pisces line of diving and snorkeling books in 1997. The series is being developed and substantially revamped over the next few years. We welcome your comments and suggestions.

## Pisces Pre-Dive Safety Guidelines

Before embarking on a scuba diving, skin diving or snorkeling trip, carefully consider the following to help ensure a safe and enjoyable experience:

- Possess a current diving certification card from a recognized scuba diving instructional agency (if scuba diving)
- Be sure you are healthy and feel comfortable diving
- Obtain reliable information about physical and environmental conditions at the dive site (e.g., from a reputable local dive operation)
- Be aware of local laws, regulations and etiquette about marine life and environment
- Dive at sites within your experience level; if possible, engage the services of a competent, professionally trained dive instructor or divemaster

Underwater conditions vary significantly from one region, or even site, to another. Seasonal changes can significantly alter site and dive conditions. These differences influence the way divers dress for a dive and what diving techniques they use.

There are special requirements for diving in any area, regardless of location. Before your dive, ask about environmental characteristics that can affect your diving and how trained local divers deal with these considerations.

---

## Warning & Request

Things change—dive site conditions, regulations, topside information. Nothing stays the same for long. Your feedback on this book will be used to help update and improve the next edition. Excerpts from your correspondence may appear in *Planet Talk*, our quarterly newsletter, or *Comet*, our monthly email newsletter. Please let us know if you do not want your letter published or your name acknowledged.

Correspondence can be addressed to:
**Lonely Planet Publications**
**Pisces Books**
150 Linden Street
Oakland, CA 94607
email: pisces@lonelyplanet.com

# Introduction

The Republic of Palau (also known as Belau) is one of diving's legendary and premier destinations. With its huge barrier reef, incredible Rock Islands, unique marine lakes and sheer drop-offs, Palau has the natural beauty and variety to excite any visitor. Just north of the equator in the western Pacific Ocean, Palau's warm tropical waters hold one of the greatest varieties of sea life found anywhere. It is famous for the schooling sharks cruising along many of the passes and corners when the current is running. It also has one of the world's largest collections of WWII shipwrecks.

The geographic variety complements the undersea terrain. It comprises high-forested islands, sparkling coral atolls and stunning limestone rock islands surrounded by fringing coral reef. The superb land diversity ranges from tiny dots of land to hulking Babeldaob, the second largest island in Micronesia. The official count says there are about 340 islands in the archipelago, but all the tiny islets and jungle-topped Rock Islands surely increase that count.

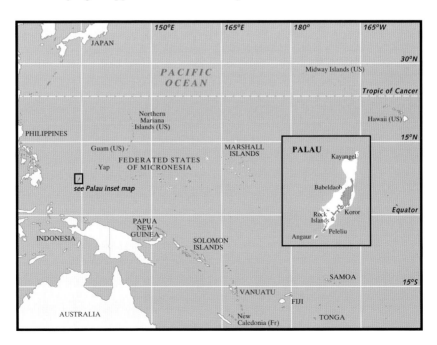

The people of Palau are perhaps among the best traveled and most adventurous of any culture in the Pacific. Seeking education, employment and adventure, many Palauans have lived elsewhere in the world. Palauans are also curious about other cultures and are very accepting of visitors. They are generally incredibly quick to converse, joke and quip.

Koror, Palau's main population center, is home to a blend of Palauan and Asian cultures. Accommodations range from first-class hotels to cozy homestays. Restaurants also reflect the cultural mix, running the gamut from local seafood establishments to ethnic eateries that include Chinese, Japanese, Thai and even Mexican food.

Out of town, quiet villages dot the shorelines of the sleepy southern islands of Angaur and Peleliu. On Babeldaob, despite its size, many coastal villages are still accessible only by boat. The rivers feed thick mazes of mangrove, creating the perfect environment for juvenile sea life. These rich nutrients also flow out onto the reef, energizing the immense coral colonies.

This book covers five dive-site regions, highlighting the best dives around Peleliu, the southern, central and northern Rock Islands, and Babeldaob and the northern reaches of the archipelago. Included are some of the world's most exciting drift dives, rarely explored shipwrecks and a handful of beautiful spots to snorkel. Full-day boat trips or longer stays on live-aboards are the most popular ways to dive here, which often means a between-dive break on the pristine beaches and uninhabited islands that simply beckon for exploration.

Eventually, even the most avid divers and snorkelers need to dry off. Other sections in this book will give you information on Palau's interesting history and culture, topside practicalities, on-land activities and attractions and a listing of diving services. Combine tropical waters, stunning underwater terrain and endless topside fun with the warm Palauan culture, and it's no wonder why Palau is a destination divers return to again and again.

Rock Island Arch is a notable landmark in Palau's Rock Islands.

Aerial view of the densely wooded Rock Islands.

# Overview

Palau is known globally as a world-class diving destination, but it also has much to offer the naturalist, historian and culture-seeker. Located about 800 miles (or roughly 1,300km) southwest of Guam in the northwest Pacific Ocean, this 100 mile- (161km-) long archipelago sits in one of the world's richest marine environments. Not only is the sea life abundant, its islands are home to flamboyant birds, monkeys and graceful flying foxes.

The Republic of Palau also includes the six Southwest Islands, about 200 miles (322km) to the southwest of the main archipelago near Philippine and Indonesian waters. The islands are sparsely populated and people mostly survive off what the island and sea provides. They speak a language closer to that of the Caroline Island Yapese. Homes are made of woven palm fronds, and islanders still practice the traditional art of canoe building. Diving is done here only by special charter and usually in the summer months when the water is calm.

Palau's population is still fairly small, under 20,000 people, most of whom live in and around Koror. The population comprises mostly Palauans, but many Filipino workers now live in Palau. Taiwanese, Japanese, Americans, Micronesians, Indonesians and some Europeans round out the mix, making Palau an interesting melting pot of cultures.

## Geography

Palau is considered one of the world's natural wonders both above and below the surface of the water. The islands represent two geologic happenings: the largest islands were formed by Eocene volcanic activity and are primarily basalt and andesite. They have a high profile with an intricate stream system and a great diversity of plant life. The rainforest is thick and in some places, difficult to penetrate.

Near the center of the country are the emerald-colored, jungled Rock Islands. These magnificent mushroom-shaped limestone formations provide a maze of splendid natural beauty and are a protected haven for many rare forms of sea life. Peleliu and Angaur in the south are low platform limestone islands, with Peleliu having a high dragonback ridge running down its spine. Kayangel, north of Babeldaob, is a classic coral atoll. Babeldaob is called a high island. It is geologically the oldest landmass in the archipelago with rolling hills, rivers and old-forest jungles. The Southwest Islands are reef flats that have been subject to uplift from the shifting of active undersea Pacific plates.

Palau is blessed with a rich diversity of biologically unique plants and animals. Tropical forest covers much of the islands, including ironwood, banyan, coconut, pandanus and broadleaf hardwood trees. Other areas feature mangrove forest and even grassland savanna. Palau has 50 species of resident birds including seabirds, land and wetland varieties. The spectacular marine environment boasts over 1,500 species of fish, over 700 species of coral and anemones and even saltwater riparian crocodiles.

Rare species, such as giant tridacna clams and dugongs (fluke-tailed manatees), are also found here. There are no poisonous animals or reptiles on Palau, except for a rarely seen jungle snake. Mammals are mostly introduced species, including monkeys, brought by the Germans to Angaur. Reptiles include the crocodiles, geckos and skinks, monitor lizards, two kinds of snakes and some large toads. Insect life is also diverse and, thankfully, there are no malarial mosquitoes.

## Seventy Islands

As you fly into Palau, you will no doubt pass over the incomparable Seventy Islands Wildlife Preserve. This group of islands, which has the soft white sand that is a natural habitat for egg-laying sea turtles, cannot be visited by water, but its mazelike channels, aquamarine water and verdant islands make them a picture postcard from the air.

# History

## Early History

Early Palauans lived an isolated existence. The islands were rich in resources so Palauans practiced terrace farming as well as fishing and hunting. Remains of the ancient terraces can still be seen on many Palauan hillsides. It is believed that because the islands were so abundant, Palauans had much time to practice artistic skills, perfect building techniques, get into politics and even war with one another. Two different chiefs traditionally ruled the north and south of the islands. That is true to this day, as traditional titles are still held by individuals and clans. The word Babeldaob—the name for the north island—means "upper ocean" and Iouldaob, the name for southern Palau, means "lower ocean."

The actual origin of the first Palauans is uncertain, but linguistic and archaeological studies show that Malays from Indonesia, Melanesians from New Guinea and some Polynesians formed the basic genetic stock, resulting in a diversity of complexion and facial types. Palauan money consisting of yellow and orange glass beads, similar to money found in Indonesia, further traces the origin of Palauans to the Malay region. Ancient village sites on the Rock Islands and the spectacular terraces on Babeldaob have been carbon dated to 1000 BC.

A Palauan woman tends her garden in Ngardma.

## European Contact

Historians estimate there were 40,000 Palauans living in the islands at the first European contact, when Capt. Henry Wilson shipwrecked the *Antelope* on

Ulong Island in 1783. The islanders lived in a thriving and complex society that was highly organized. Still true today, women had an important advisory role and influential control over land and money. Studies show that Palau's pre-European-contact population was much larger than at any other time in its history.

The British controlled trade with Palau until 1885, when the Spanish took over until 1899. Christianity became a strong influence in Palauan lives, and European diseases took their toll. The population dwindled during the next century. By 1900 there were only 4,000 Palauans left.

The Germans bought Palau and the rest of the Caroline Islands after Spain lost the Spanish-American War in 1899. German administrators introduced modern methods for stemming the spread of disease, which was a blessing to the dwindling Palauan population.

## Japanese Occupation

Japan took control of the islands in 1914 and ruled them until the end of WWII. The Japanese built the islands into progressive and productive communities that specialized in mining, agriculture and fishing. When the war came, the islands were heavily fortified.

Angaur and Peleliu were the settings for fierce battles; the one on tiny Peleliu lasted for three bloody months. Months before, a two-day air strike sank a major block of the Japanese fleet, and you can still see the war remnants today. Koror was wiped out after U.S. forces took control of the islands.

The job of rebuilding the pre-war intricate and productive Japanese infrastructure continues. The older people of Palau speak Japanese and sing Japanese songs when reminiscing.

## Trust Territory

After the war, the UN established the Trust Territory of the Pacific, which included the Northern Marianas, Pohnpei, Chuuk, Yap, Kosrae, the Marshall Islands and Palau. Under UN guidelines, the U.S. was obliged to foster the development of political and economic institutions, with the ultimate goal of helping Micronesians achieve self-sufficiency.

As years passed, the U.S. minimalist approach to governing the islands irritated many island leaders. Most islands broke free to form their own independent state or nation. Still, in one form or another, all of the islands are associated with the U.S. The U.S. allows the nations to use its currency and postal system and provides access to certain federal programs and military protection.

In return, it asks that in time of military crisis it be allowed to establish bases on the islands. Palau's insistence that no nuclear armaments be brought into the country (bolstered by an amendment to its 1979 constitution) brought on the longest and most protracted negotiations of any of the Micronesian islands. The proposal to put a nuclear submarine base in Babeldaob led to Palau making appeals before the UN to stop the project. Feelings ran hot in the country. Bloodshed, arson and intense politics resulted. Endless debates ensued and eight elections were held in the 1980s and '90s to ratify the ever-changing Compact of Free Association between Palau and the U.S. By 1990, Palau had become the last trust territory in the world.

Finally the new Compact of Free Association was approved in 1994. Palau's wait netted it the largest use settlement of any Micronesian island nation: $450 million in aid over the first 15 years of the agreement. Palau was recognized as a UN member in December 1994. Today, Palau's government attempts to retain traditional values and roles by melding them with modern politics.

## Culture Corner

Palauans have lived in the archipelago since 1000 BC, and in that time have developed a distinct culture, still expressed through dance, music, myths and legends, depicted in intricately carved wooden storyboards and woven artifacts. *Abai*, or public meeting houses, are still found in Koror, Kayangel and Airai, and offer tantalizing insights into Palauan society.

By European contact in 1783, Palauans already had a sophisticated and complex social organization. Palauan society was centered on one theme: competition for money, prestige and power, which was gained through political power within a clan or village. This competition was channeled into activities such as sports, politics and war.

Tattooed Palauan men wore their hair in tight buns. *Rubak* (important chiefs) wore bracelets made from dugong vertebrae. Fishing was their livelihood. Inter-village wars were common, and men spent much of their time mastering the art of house and canoe building and refining their use of tools and weapons.

Women were also tattooed; the design was especially ornate on women of high clans. *Rubak'l Dil* (important women of the clan) wielded much power and they still do today. They excelled at agriculture, primarily the cultivation of taro, the village's staple food. Their role as food producers conferred upon them a superior social status and political position.

The ornate interior carvings of Airai Abai.

134°15'E  134°30'E

Ngerechur
Ngerkeklau
Arukofon Point
*Ngos Reef*

## Republic Of Palau

8°N   132°E   Kayangel
Babeldaob
Koror
Peleliu
Angaur
**See Main Map**

Sonsorol
Islands

Pulo Anna

Merir

4°N

Tobi   Helen

0   100   200 km
0   50   100 miles

Kepulauan Asia
(Indonesia)

*Ngertoell Reef*

**Devilfish City**
Current-swept channel and
manta ray cleaning station

*Ngerdmaru Bay*

*Aiyasu Reef*

*Ngeremlengui Pass*

Babeldaob   7°30'N

*Idims Reef*

*Ngenelachel Passage*

*Dibard Reef*

*PHILIPPINE SEA*

*Ngetngod Reef*

**Siaes Tunnel**
ammoth deepwater hole combines
beauty and deep sea mystery

## Chandelier Cave
Dripstone formations and air chambers
make this a favorite novelty dive

Ngerekebesang   Koror
✈ Palau Airport
Malakal   Orrak
*Malakal Harbor*

### *Iro Maru*
Prolific coral growth and an intact
bow gun on this WWII wreck

Ulong Island

Ngeruktabel   Ulebsechel

**Helmet Wreck**
Unidentified WWII wreck with treasure
trove of war materials and artifacts

*Cchelbeluu Reef*   7°15'N

## Ngerumekaol Pass
High-voltage drift dive near tropical
paradise of Ulong Island

Urukthapel

## Blue Corner & Blue Holes
metimes crowded, these famed sites
re unrivalled for sizzling fish action

Ngerukeuid

## Jellyfish Lake
Snorkeling with thousands of stingless
jellies is a sensual and surreal experience

Mecherchar
*Chudel Reef*

Ngemelis
*German Channel*
Cheleu   Ngercheu
*Denges Passage*
Ngerchong

*NORTH PACIFIC OCEAN*

## Big Drop-Off
hallow waters leading to plunging
byss attracts snorkelers and divers

Oingenaol
Ngedbus
*Ngetbar Reef*

0   5   10 km
0   3   6 miles
*not for navigation*   7°00'N

Peleliu   Ngebad

## Peleliu Wall & Tip
Huge gorgonians, black coral and big-fish
action converge at this current-swept site

Angaur

Reef
Elevation
600ft
450ft
300ft
150ft
Sea Level

134°15'E   134°30'E

# Practicalities

## Climate

Palau's location, 7°30'N north latitude, 133°30'E longitude, makes it a very tropical place. Despite a distinct rainy season and occasional winds, diving here is a year-round activity. Rainy season is September through November, with showers possible starting in June. During this period, squalls may blow in for a couple of days but are quickly followed by sunny skies and calm seas. The trade winds blow starting in January, usually ending by May, but most dive sites are sheltered by the islands. Air temperatures vary from lows of 76°F (24°C) at night to possible highs of 90°F (32°C) during the day. Average temperature is a comfortable 86°F (30°C). The average water temperature varies slightly from about 78 to 82°F (26 to 28°C).

# Language

Both English and Palauan are official languages. English is more common in business and government, and Palauan is spoken at home. Many elderly people are fluent in

## Pocket Palauan

| English | Palauan | Pronunciation |
| --- | --- | --- |
| hello | alii | ah-LEE |
| goodbye | mechikung | May-ee-gong |
| how are you? | ke ua ngerang? | ka-wannga-RANGH |
| I'm well (thanks) | ak mesisiich (sulang) | |
| good morning | ungil tutau | oong-EEL-too-TAW |
| good afternoon | ungil chodechosong | oong-EEL OTH-o-song |
| good evening | ungil kebesengei | oong-EEL-kebba sung Ay |
| please. | adang | Ah-DAHNG |
| thanks | sulang | soo-LAHNG |
| I am leaving | ak morolung | ahk-more-oh-long |
| what is your name? | ngtecha ngklem? | ngte-AHNG-KLEMM |
| my name is ____ | a ngklek a ____ | Ahng-KLEKK-a ____ |
| what is the price? | ngteland a cheral? | ngtela-ah-RAHL |
| yes | choi, o' oi | OH-OY |
| no | ng diak | Inh-dee-AHK |
| stop, that's enough! | merkong! | Murr-GONG |

Japanese, reflective of Palau's days as a Japanese possession prior to WWII. There is still an afternoon radio hour that plays old Japanese songs to bring back memories of those affluent days. Southwest Islanders speak Sonsorolese and Tobian languages, which are more closely related to Yapese or Chuukese than to Palauan.

A Palauan woman instructs her granddaughter in the art of traditional weaving.

# Getting There

Direct flights to Palau are available via Manila (Philippines), or from the U.S. and Japan via Guam on Continental Airlines (☎ 680-488-2448 in Koror). A number of weekly flights connect Palau with other metropolitan Asian cities. Coming from the Southern Hemisphere, connections to Guam can be made at Melbourne or Brisbane, Australia. Air Nauru (☎ 671-649-7106 in Guam) also has a Manila-Guam connection. Travelers can then connect to Continental's Palau legs. The airport is in Airai State, in southern Babeldaob, a 25-minute drive from central Koror.

# Gateway City – Koror

Koror is Palau's main commercial and political center and is also where most of the visiting divers stay, eat and party. Most places in Koror can be visited on foot and the streets are virtually crime free, so walking around even in the evening is no problem.

A number of historic sites in the city display remnants of the Japanese occupation during WWII. Stately lion statue carvings and other vestiges of the Japanese occupation can be seen along the roads. In the 1920s and 1930s Koror had three times the population it has now, which hovers around 10,000 people.

Nightlife includes a number of good restaurants featuring a host of ethnic foods, karaoke bars for the golden throated and some good local bars for those who love to cha-cha. Airline ticketing offices, postal facilities and department stores are all centrally located in downtown Koror. One warning: traffic (by Palau standards) gets heavy during rush hours.

Koror once had a midnight curfew to ensure that bars closed and people came home to bed. This midnight curfew law changes frequently, as nighttime flights mean people have to drive around after midnight. Koror nightlifers should ask if the curfew is in effect when planning on staying out late. There is also a 9pm curfew for teens, though it is poorly enforced.

The **Palau Visitors Authority** (☎ 680-488-2793) is the national agency in charge of assisting visitors during their stay in Palau. You'll find it at the T-intersection next to the stoplight that leads to the road to Meyuns. Open from 9am to 5pm on weekdays, the people are very helpful and can supply information on every tourism-related business in Palau.

## Koror State

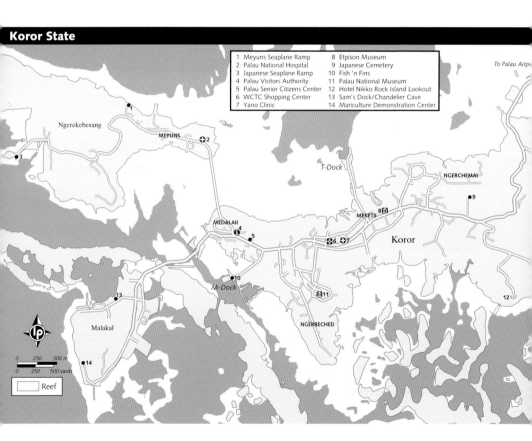

| 1 Meyuns Seaplane Ramp | 8 Etpison Museum |
| 2 Palau National Hospital | 9 Japanese Cemetery |
| 3 Japanese Seaplane Ramp | 10 Fish 'n Fins |
| 4 Palau Visitors Authority | 11 Palau National Museum |
| 5 Palau Senior Citizens Center | 12 Hotel Nikko Rock Island Lookout |
| 6 WCTC Shopping Center | 13 Sam's Dock/Chandelier Cave |
| 7 Yano Clinic | 14 Mariculture Demonstration Center |

A street scene and market in downtown Koror.

# Getting Around

Taxis are plentiful and can be called to most locations. Local cab drivers are usually dependable, colorful characters. When you go out at night, you can arrange to be dropped off and picked up later, but make sure you know how much you're paying for this convenience prior to making the deal. Taxi prices are not overly expensive so don't expect to pay what you pay in big cities or even Guam.

Cars, local boats and buses are also available to rent through your hotel and at rental booths at the airport. Your dive shop can arrange a private boat, but a boat driver is necessary as Palau has many tricky reefs and a 6 to 7ft tide change.

Colorful flowers line Palau's roads and walkways.

Larger hotels and dive shops provide transportation to their dive boats, to town and to the airport for $5 to $15 each way, depending on where you are going. Check with your dive shop to see if they'll come get you in the morning and drop you off in the afternoon.

# Entry

Proof of citizenship (passport or birth certificate) is required for U.S. citizens. Entry or travel visas are not required. Non-U.S. citizens must have a valid passport. All visitors must possess a return or onward ticket. The Chief of Immigration must approve any stay beyond 30 days, for which there is a fee of $100.

Yellow fever and cholera immunizations are required for anyone arriving from infected areas.

A departure tax of $20 is payable upon check-in at the airport. Keep some cash on hand, as you cannot use credit cards to pay the tax. In order to get into the departure lounge, the receipt showing you paid the tax must be attached to your boarding pass.

# Time

Palau is on the western side of the international dateline, which means you lose a day if you're coming from points east. Palau is 9 hours ahead of GMT. When it's noon in Palau, it is 1pm in Sydney, 3am in London and 7pm the day before in San Francisco. Daylight saving is not observed.

# Money

The U.S. dollar is the official currency and several U.S. banks operate in Palau. Major credit cards are welcome at most visitor-oriented businesses. You can get cash from credit cards at the banks and at automatic teller machines, which are found in Koror. Foreign currency exchange is a hassle, however, so try to bring U.S. dollars. Banking hours are weekdays 10am to 3pm, with some banks open later on paydays or Fridays.

# Electricity

Standard electricity is 110/120V, 60 cycles, with U.S.-type two-pronged plugs. Adapters and converters aren't readily available for those with 220V systems, so bring your own if you need to convert.

# Weights & Measures

The U.S. imperial system of weights and measures is used throughout the islands. All sale and rental dive gear is oriented this way—depths are measured in feet, weights in pounds and compressed air is measured in pounds-per-square inch (psi). In this book, both imperial and metric measurements are given, except for specific references to depth within the dive site descriptions, which are given in feet. See the conversion chart in the back of this book for metric and imperial equivalents.

# What to Bring

## General

It never gets cold in Palau, so bring only lightweight clothing. Casual island style prevails, although visitors are strongly advised to respect the local customs by not wearing swimsuits, short-shorts or other inappropriate clothing in town, villages or public buildings. Women should wear a sarong or skirt to cover their thighs. Swimsuits are fine on the boats and on the "lunch islands." Hats, sunglasses and sunscreen are highly recommended, especially on boats, as the water is very reflective.

## Dive-Related

For diving, a dive skin or 1 to 3mm wetsuit is all you'll need. It's always best to bring your own dive gear, though high-quality gear is available to rent from most dive shops. Extra weights and belts are usually brought on boat trips, so do not lug these along. Equipment servicing is available for certain gear, primarily for brands manufactured in the U.S. Bring a rain slicker or light parka on the boat, as a cool rain after a dive can be a bit chilly.

# Underwater Photography

Palau's live-aboards and some of the larger dive operations rent still or video cameras and related gear, such as strobes and lenses. Many can also provide personalized training and advanced instruction, or you can hire one of the excellent photo pros to photograph your dives.

Underwater photo equipment sales are uncommon, but you can find some items. Batteries, including good alkalines, are readily available. If you are serious about shooting in Palau, it is best to bring everything you need. **KD Photo** at **Sam's Dive Tours** is a good place to go for repairs.

Purchase slide and print film at the pro shops and on the live-aboards. E6 processing is available at KD Photo, **NECO Marine** and **Photo Palau** (at **Splash Diving Center**), and on the *Aggressor*, *Sundancer* and *Ocean Hunter* live-aboards. C46 print film is also processed at many venues in town. Digital prints and system processing is not available.

A photographer "gets close and shoots up" at an obliging Napoleon wrasse.

# Business Hours

Business hours are usually weekdays from 8am to noon and 1 to 5pm. On weekends most retail outlets are open, but some limit hours to 8:30am to 1:30pm. Banks and government offices are closed on weekends. Restaurants and bars are open daily. Restaurants close about 10pm with bars open until midnight, though occasionally a bartender will keep the bar open later (past curfew) if it is hopping.

# Telecommunications/Postal

Palau uses the U.S. postal system but has its own stamps. The main post office is in downtown Koror and is open daily from 8am to 4pm, 9 to 10am Saturday and closed Sundays and holidays. Palau stamps and sets are available and considered quite collectable.

There is a communication station run by the national government and some independent telephone and computer companies in Koror. Through them, world-wide telephone, facsimile, telex, IDD, Internet/email service and operator-assisted dialing services are available. If you really don't want to get away from it all, there are three radio stations, 12 TV channels and CNN broadcasts 24 hours a day.

Local newspapers include the weekly *Palau Horizon* and the bi-weekly *Tia Belau*. The only daily is Guam's *Pacific Daily News*.

# Accommodations

Palau has accommodations for every budget and taste. You can find everything from full-service resorts and moderately priced bungalows to economical motels or homestays. Most of these are based out of Koror, although local tour operators can help you arrange to camp on the Rock Islands. You can also make arrangements through the Palau Visitors Authority to stay in local homes or rustic resorts on far off islands. See the Activities & Attractions section for information on island camping.

Palau Pacific Resort, just outside of Koror, and Carp Island Resort are currently the only dedicated dive resorts in Palau. Most dive shops have package deals that include accommodations, and some of the nicer hotels include airport pick-up. See the Listings section for accommodations contact information.

# Dining & Food

Dining in Palau's restaurants offers an eclectic mix of cuisine and tastes. Fresh local seafood is the star on many menus and you can choose exotic local dishes as well as the ubiquitous pizza, or traditional Japanese, Chinese, Mexican or even

American fare. There are open-air cocktail lounges, some offering live entertainment or karaoke for those not too tired from a day of diving.

Tasting fine seafood cuisine in the many local restaurants is a must. Sashimi, fish dinners and local dishes are available at a number of places in and around Koror. If you find a restaurant you like, ask them to make arrangements for a meal of mangrove crab.

For food and water to eat on the dive boats or in the rooms, the local stores sell bottled water, soft drinks and alcoholic drinks. Most dive operators prepare sandwiches or bento boxes, which is a Japanese term for an assortment takeout. The **WCTC grocery** store in the Ben Franklin shopping center has a deli and nearby the **Yano Store** sells local specialties. Good meals to go can also be found at **Happy Landing** on the way to Malakal.

# Shopping

The most sought after art form in Palau, next to the T-shirt, is undoubtedly the storyboard. Storyboards are sold at many stores and even at the Koror jail. Also popular are woven items, postcards and posters, books and some local artwork.

The largest department store in Koror, **Ben Franklin**, has a large souvenir department and across the street, **Surangel's** is also well stocked with T-shirts and various items. A block away, the Palau Shop has a nice collection of clothing and you can make your own personalized Palau T-shirt using various stock designs. **George Ngiraisaol Gift Shop** next to the Yano Clinic usually has

Francisco, a well-known storyboard carver, working on a new creation.

a good storyboard selection at reasonable prices. Pricier but good quality storyboards are also sold at **Duty Free Shoppers** in the Palau Pacific Resort and Palasia Resort.

At the Senior Citizens Center across from the court house, elderly men and women pool their collective talents to preserve the arts and culture of Palau. The center features the **Ormuul Gift Shop**, where unique, handmade items by local artisans include woven bags, jewelry and carved storyboards.

## Turtle & Black-Coral Products: To Buy or Not to Buy?

A few stores in Palau sell turtle and black-coral products. The use of turtle shell in traditional women's money is still a strong cultural norm. But these pieces are highly valued, individually produced, and remain in the local families. The making of these money pieces is a time-honored tradition and not common nowadays.

The turtle shell used to produce jewelry found in Palau's stores was probably taken against local and international law. But the laws are not strongly enforced in Palau, and some stores still sell these objects in the form of bracelets, earrings, rings and hair adornments. Be aware before you buy turtle products that all eight species of the world's sea turtles are either endangered or threatened. Activities contributing to the demise of these creatures include: hunting for human consumption, production of turtle-shell jewelry and ornaments, loss of habitat due to tourism and development, and injury from ship propellers and boat traffic.

Also increasingly under pressure, black coral tends to grow in deep water and, because it is hard to get at, it is considered a somewhat valuable material. Appearing more golden than black underwater, when polished to a glossy black finish the coral is often fashioned into jewelry.

Unfortunately, black coral is still sold locally. Visitors can help discourage the depletion of wild black coral by taking only photographs and by not purchasing black-coral souvenirs.

Many countries do not allow the importation of turtle-shell or black-coral materials, so ask if you don't know what something is made of. Be sure to tell the store owner if you do not approve of the sale of products made from endangered species.

# Activities & Attractions

There are plenty of things to do in Palau besides dive. Aside from the activities described below, touristy attractions like jet skiing, banana boat rides and parasailing are also available. However, ecotourism-oriented activities are highly encouraged as a way to enjoy and respect the environment. Similarly, in most areas, the taking of shells and natural artifacts is strictly prohibited.

## Exploring Babeldaob

Activities on Babeldaob take a little more energy to arrange, but they are well worth it if you don't mind roughing it a bit to experience something completely different. Trips here aren't heavily organized, so be prepared to roll with the punches a little.

Many dive shops can arrange a trip with a local guide. Remember, Babeldaob is the second largest island in Micronesia but has little infrastructure, so many of these excursions take the whole day. A boat ride up the coast followed by a hike or a rather bouncy truck ride on largely unpaved roads are the norm for folks visiting Babeldaob. Some people use rented 4-wheel-drives to go it on their own. Regardless, remember to bring plenty of water and some snacks as there are no restaurants along the road.

Hiking is popular, especially at the waterfalls. A favorite route is the hike to the **Ngardmau Falls**, which follows a canopied jungle path across rivers and into the northern hills. The falls flow from Palau's tallest peak, 713ft- (217m-) high Mount Ngerchelechuus. They are at their best after a rain and the hiking is coolest when it is raining, so moisture from the sky shouldn't deter eager hikers. There are also other falls on this island, such as the popular **Ngatpang Waterfall**.

Other sites on Babeldaob record the island's ancient history or tell of legends. The **Badrulchau Stone Monoliths** sit way up north on the grassy flats along the eastern coastline of Ngarchelong. There are 37 ancient stone monoliths, whose origins remain unknown. According to one version, the pillars are actually the foundation of a Bai meeting house that was being built by the gods. The **Stone Faces of Ollei** in northern Babeldaob are a must for anyone wanting to see the "Easter Island of Micronesia."

The **Ngermeskang River** in central Babeldaob is an unspoiled beauty. Ranging in habitat from a mangrove forest at its coastal mouth to a dense jungle farther inland, this river is wonderful for nature lovers and adventure seekers alike. Look for the remnants of the Japanese pineapple cannery far upriver, where wild pineapples still grow. This is where kayakers paddle up-river from the river mouth. If you're stealthy, you can sneak up on saltwater crocodiles.

The **Ancient Ruins of Imeungs** are found on a hill that is embraced by a ridge of mountains on the southwestern portion of Babeldaob. Imeungs was once the political and military center of the area. There are stone pathways, stone foundations and a natural amphitheater where young warriors once tested their mettle by trying to leap a waist-high stone.

**Lake Ngerdok** is both Palau's largest freshwater reservoir and the largest sanctuary for crocodiles. Adventurous naturalists can hike a trail to the lake for a glimpse. Bring binoculars, as the crocs are generally shy of people.

Painted legends and a glimpse into the past can be found at the **Melekeok Bai** and the **Airai Bai**. These meeting houses were once extremely common and found in every village and community. Both have painted gables telling of past glories; some even poke fun at the other villages.

A short climb into the Rock Islands of Babeldaob brings you to **Metuker ra Bisech**. These quarry caves are where people from the neighboring islands of Yap once traveled some 400 miles (644km) over open ocean in outrigger canoes to mine quartz for their famous stone money. These wheel-like pieces of stone sometimes measured more than a yard or meter in diameter. Some of these heavy disks still sit in the jungle.

The Ollei stone faces are reminiscent of Easter Island's giant statues.

Yapese sailors in outrigger canoes came to Palau to mine quartz for their stone money.

# Exploring Other Islands

Even though Babeldaob is the biggest and most-hikeable area, there's a lot of exploring to do on the other islands. In Koror, you can follow stone paths in ancient villages to taro patches and venues along the sea. One of the easiest to find is just past the Nikko Hotel in **Ngermid**.

Wreckage of a WWII Japanese airplane is still evident on Angaur.

WWII buffs may want to explore the hills of **Peleliu Island**, which are full of old war memorabilia. Some ammunition may be still active, so watch your step. War monuments and bat-filled caves are found around various battle sites.

South, on **Angaur Island**, you'll find more WWII remnants strewn across the island. Also check out the jungle past the Santa Maria statue, where an old phosphate mine is fun to explore. At certain times of day, you can find it full of monkeys.

**Carp Island** also has some nice hikes. Nestled in the southern Rock Islands, its quiet beaches and towering trees greet the jungle trekker.

# Running

For those who want to combine socializing with a jungle jog, the **Palau Hash House Harriers** meet every other Saturday in front of the post office at about 3pm. This loosely organized fun bunch sets a hound-and-hare run and provides snacks and beer afterward for a small fee. It's a good way to meet some of the local folks in a relaxed setting.

Before setting off into the jungle, be warned that a particular species of tree growing here exudes a black sap. If that gets on you it burns like crazy and can be difficult to treat. Yano's clinic has seen a lot of this, so if you inadvertently touch one of these trees, go see Dr. Yano as soon as possible.

# Kayaking

If you want to add an exciting notch in your kayak belt, Palau is the place to do it. This huge archipelago offers some of the most diverse and challenging kayaking

Ocean kayaking around the Rock Islands is an ideal way to explore.

conditions in Micronesia. If heavy currents, big waves and vast tide changes aren't enough to contend with, try fending off a saltwater crocodile with your paddle!

Palau has tours and combined hikes for virtually every level of water enthusiast. The highlight of most of the tours is, of course, the fantastic Rock Islands. The topography of the Rock Islands or the inner causeways of Babeldaob's rivers and mangroves ensure an amazing time, whether it be a half-day jaunt or a half-month adventure.

Ron Leidich, who set up **Planet Blue Kayak Tours** at Sam's Dive Tours in Koror, brings years of experience as a professional land and marine biologist, and trained river and diving guide. This makes him and his other trained naturalists interesting guides to take a paddle with. Destinations include Nikko Bay, Tarzan Cave, Jurassic Lake and lots of other strange and incredible natural sites that are only reachable by kayak.

## Traditional Outrigger Canoe Trips

Fish N' Fins offers a unique paddling experience using handmade canoes, which are replicas of Palau's old war canoes. The guides are local and the tour goes to places through the Rock Islands where dive boats don't go.

Billed as a total eco-experience, the boats take no plastic on board. The food is local fare wrapped in banana leaves and accompanied by fresh fruits, coconuts and water, all packed in a local basket.

On an average half-day tour you'll paddle through WWII relics, fresh-water springs and bat caves. Your guide will point out special medicinal plants, and will take you to fish nursery areas. This silent paddle trip even gets to areas where you'll have a chance to see a dugong or a crocodile.

Trips can be arranged anytime—you can go for a few hours, or a full day with overnight camping. Each canoe takes up to five people. On full-moon nights, a moonlit paddle through the labyrinth comes complete with wine, cheese and crackers.

Palau's sturdy war canoes were intricately decorated.

Special tours include a trip to an old Japanese WWII settlement high atop an emerald Rock Island. Your guide will point out flora and fauna, while telling you about Palau's war history. Another trip takes you to Long Lake, where a ride on the rushing current takes you through a crystal clear mangrove channel. This channel leads to a unique marine lake filled with giant clams, turtles and eagle rays. Pacific white birds soar overhead.

Another trip goes to an ancient Palauan burial cave, where stalactites still drip. Others show you intricate Palauan art. The Tarzan tour is just plain fun, with rope swings, cliff jumps and cave dives. It includes paddling into a lake that is home to a monster barracuda. This is an extreme daytrip. The even more adventurous can arrange a two-day or two-week trip, depending on your fitness and experience level.

# Camping in the Rock Islands

Palau's Rock Islands are possibly the best place for camping in all of Micronesia and, for those who don't mind roughing it a little, an experience not to be missed. The lapping of the waves on shore, the setting tropical sun, the nighttime noises of the nesting birds and the carpet of stars that lines the sky are all unforgettable sights and sounds, and perhaps best appreciated while on your own deserted island.

Some of the Rock Islands have been set up for camping, with very basic toilet facilities and shelters, though none have water. Other islands are undeveloped (and uninhabited), but a jug of fresh water, a tent and a mattress are all you'll need to spend a night or two on an island.

You can also combine camping with diving. With sufficient advance notice, many of the dive operations will drop you off and pick you up at a pre-arranged time, in conjunction with a dive group. For maximum solitude and self-sufficiency, you can make your dives and then be dropped off at an island afterward, and be left to your own devices. The next morning the boat can pick you up for more diving. If you need a little more personal attention, a guide can be arranged, and can help with catching and cooking fish and making sure you don't pitch your tent where the tide comes in.

Be aware that "Rock Island squirrels," otherwise known as common island rats, may emerge at night on some of the islands. They are harmless, but may try to get into your food if it is left out unprotected. Also, on islands with large land crab populations, a full moon can be both amazing and eerie as they all come out on the beach. On breezy nights, mosquitoes are rarely a problem; otherwise a good repellent keeps them at bay. Fires are permitted and add great atmosphere to the campout, although they certainly aren't needed for warmth. A fresh fish cooked over the open fire is a real treat.

Planet Blue Kayak Tours at Sam's Dive Tours can rent you all the necessary gear, whether you want to camp for a day or a month. Diving and kayaking tours can also be combined and Sam often leads specialized fishing and diving campouts to places like Turtle Cove, Peleliu and even Kayangel Atoll. **Island Nation** also has some nice trips to the northern islands around Ngerchelong in Babeldaob. Owner Jimmy Kloulechad can arrange for you to stay in a small barrack at the dock area, or you can stay on the beaches of neighboring islands, where the only possible distraction is the squealing of wild pigs.

Camp on your own beach on one of the Rock Islands.

# Birding

Palau has a great variety of bird life. There are 50 species of resident birds including seabirds, land and wetland varieties. The northern atoll islands attract seabirds like frigates and noddies, while the interior jungles are home to the Palauan pigeon, a tiny forest owl and kingfishers. Look for boobies, cockatoos and parrots in the Rock Islands. Palau's local conservation groups and the government's wildlife division have detailed information on Palau's endemic and rare species.

# Fishing

Fishing in Palau is quite good and Palauan men take great pride in being skilled fishermen. Everything from light tackle casting for jacks to angling for giants like Pacific blue marlin is found in Palau. Palau's barrier and patch reef systems make fishing and boating tricky. Locals become familiar with the complex currents, tides and channels to gain an understanding of migration and spawning patterns. The old folks attempt to pass this vast body of knowledge to the young. A series of taboos, called *rul*, are also in place to ensure certain species do not become over-fished.

Fishing charters for visitors can be arranged through many of the major dive shops. Spearfishing, line fishing, net fishing and traditional traps are also practiced though, for tourists, spearing is not encouraged and is pretty much left to the locals who spear for food. Most forms of fishing are banned near the popular dive and spawning sites.

One unique outer island fishing method involves creating a kite from a leaf, then dangling bait from a hook attached to the kite. The bobbing of the kite signals a fish on the line.

# Sailing

Sail charters through the Rock Islands can take you out for the day or longer. As you silently cruise through the protected lagoon, unimpeded by the whine of a motor, the sights and sounds of the environment embrace you. For lunch, anchor in a sandy bottom cove where you can snorkel or kayak as the crew prepares a delicious meal. With **Palau Sail Charters**, the captain usually insists that you do some of the steering, so you can truthfully say you sailed Palau.

# Mariculture Demonstration Center

At the end of the road on Malakal Island, the Palau Mariculture Demonstration Center has long, shallow tanks of giant tridacna clams. It is the world's first and largest giant-clam hatchery. Lucky clams get replanted on Palau's reefs and unlucky ones become sashimi. The PMDC also operates other aquaculture programs that have included a hawksbill turtle hatchery, trochus research and various fish food breeding programs. Stop in and see what's currently being studied. The center is open to visitors from 8 to 11am, and 1 to 4pm weekdays.

# Belau National Museum

This small building in Koror is the local treasury of historical and cultural artifacts. It offers a glimpse into Palau's rich past. The more than 1,000 objects housed here include Palauan beads and shell money, costumes, domestic utensils, weapons, tools and ornaments. In the lobby of the museum, a gift shop and bookstore offer a large selection of distinctly Palauan gifts and souvenirs.

# Diving Health & Safety

## General Health

Palau is generally a healthy place to visit. There are no malarial mosquitoes and no tropical diseases. Palau has two private medical clinics and a public hospital that has a modern, dual-lock recompression chamber.

Occasionally, Palau experiences outbreaks of dengue fever, a mosquito-spread disease like malaria, with similar symptoms such as fever, headache and severe joint and muscle pain. Unfortunately there is no prophylactic available but, although dengue fever can be dangerous to infants or elderly people, serious complications are not common. See Dr. Yano at his clinic as he has had the most local experience in treating the malady.

Tap water is drinkable in some hotels, but it's always best to ask first. Bottled water is also readily available and is often provided by dive operators.

The U.S. Center for Disease Control and Prevention regularly posts updates on health-related concerns around the world, specifically for travelers. Contact the CDC or visit their website. Call (toll-free from the U.S.) ☎ 888-232-3299 and request Document 000005 to receive a list of documents available by fax. The website is www.cdc.gov.

## Pre-Trip Preparation

Your general state of health, diving skill level and specific equipment needs are the three most important factors that impact any dive trip. If you honestly assess these before you leave, you'll be well on your way to assuring a safe dive trip.

First, if you're not in shape, start exercising. Second, if you haven't dived for a while (six months is too long) and your skills are rusty, do a local dive with an experienced buddy or take a scuba review course. Feeling good physically, diving with experience and with reliable equipment will not only increase your safety, but will also enhance your enjoyment underwater.

At least a month before your trip, inspect your dive gear. Remember, your regulator should be serviced annually. If you use a dive computer and can replace the battery yourself, change it before the trip or buy a spare one to take along. Otherwise, send the computer to the manufacturer for a battery replacement.

Purchase any additional equipment you might need, such as a dive light and tank marker light for night diving, a line reel for wreck diving, etc. Make sure you have at least a whistle attached to your BC. Better yet, add a safety sausage (also known as a marker tube or come-to-me).

## Ciguatera Poisoning

Ciguatera is a type of food poisoning with potentially serious and long-lasting effects that occurs when someone ingests sufficient amounts of toxin-laden fish. The toxin accumulates when normally safe-to-eat herbivorous fish ingest the ciguatera microorganism, commonly found living in algae and sea plants growing in coral rubble areas. The microorganism flourishes when the area is disturbed. This can be caused by things like storms, El Niño temperature fluctuations, coastal development and human pollution.

The microorganism secretes ciguatoxin, which is not fatal to the creature but is stored in the organs. When a smaller creature is eaten by a larger fish, the toxin invades the next host. Thus large and older eels, great barracuda, groupers, snappers and other major players in the upper food chain are often the most toxic and common carriers. When it enters the human system, the toxin affects neurological, gastrointestinal and cardiovascular systems. Some symptoms are similar to DCS and thus, ciguatoxin poisoning must be considered when treating bends cases.

The first symptoms generally appear two to 20 hours after eating the contaminated fish. Digestive upsets, itching, lip numbness, irregular heartbeat and sensory and neurological disorders are characteristic symptoms, and can range from mild to severe. Some are long-term and life-changing depending on the individual's reaction. A few fatalities have been attributed to the toxin in the Pacific region.

Immediate medical treatment is of utmost importance. Mannitol, an intravenous solution, is highly regarded and can be effective when used early on.

There aren't many reported cases of ciguatera in Palau, so don't be paranoid. Ciguatera-laden fish look and taste normal, and the toxin is unaffected by cooking. The best strategy is to avoid eating them in the first place. In an area reported to be infected with ciguatera, check with the inhabitants of the atoll, who know which species are diseased and the places to avoid fishing for them.

JEAN-BERNARD CARILLET

## Diving & Flying

Divers in Palau arrive by plane. While it's fine to dive soon *after* flying, it's important to remember that your last dive should be completed at least 12 hours (some experts advise 24 hours, particularly after repetitive dives) *before* your flight to minimize the risk of decompression sickness, caused by residual nitrogen in the blood.

About a week before taking off, do a final check of your gear, grease o-rings, check batteries and assemble a save-a-dive kit. This kit should at minimum contain extra mask and fin straps, snorkel keeper, mouthpiece, valve cap, zip ties and o-rings. Don't forget to pack a first-aid kit and medications such as decongestants, ear drops, antihistamines and seasickness tablets.

# Signaling Devices

Occasionally a diver becomes lost or is left behind at a dive site—make sure this never happens to you! In Palau, many dives are drift dives, where you jump in off the boat quite a ways from where the boat picks you up. A diver is extremely difficult to locate in the water, so always dive with a signaling device of some sort, preferably more than one.

SARAH J. H. HUBBARD

One of the best signaling devices and the easiest to carry is a whistle. Even the little ones are extremely effective. Use a zip tie to attach one to your BC. Even better, though more expensive, is a loud bullhorn that connects to the inflator hose. You simply push a button to let out a blast, though it does require air from your tank to function.

In order to be seen as well as heard, you should also carry a safety sausage (also called a marker tube or come-to-me). The best ones are bright in color and about 10ft (3m) high. They roll up and can easily fit into a BC pocket or be clipped

A diver demonstrates the use of a safety sausage.

onto a D-ring. They're inflated orally or with a regulator. Some allow you to insert a dive light into the tube—a nice feature when you're diving at night.

# DAN

Divers Alert Network (DAN) is an international membership association of individuals and organizations sharing a common interest in diving and safety. It includes DAN Southeast Asia and Pacific (DAN SEAP), an autonomous non-profit organization based in Australia. DAN operates a 24-hour diving emergency hotline. DAN SEAP members should call ☎ **61 8 8212 9242**. DAN America members should call ☎ **919-684-8111 or 919-684-4DAN** (-4326). The latter accepts collect calls in a dive emergency.

Though DAN does not directly provide medical care, it does provide advice on early treatment, evacuation and hyperbaric treatment of diving-related injuries. Divers should contact DAN for assistance as soon as a diving emergency is suspected.

DAN membership is reasonably priced and includes DAN TravelAssist, a membership benefit that covers medical air evacuation from anywhere in the world for any illness or injury. For a small additional fee, divers can get secondary insurance coverage for decompression illness. For membership questions, contact DAN at ☎ 800-446-2671 in the U.S. or ☎ 919-684-2948 elsewhere. DAN can also be reached at www.diversalertnetwork.org.

# Medical & Recompression Facilities

Palau has two private medical clinics and the Belau National Hospital, which is on Ngerekebesang Island just over the causeway from Koror. The hospital houses Palau's only recompression chamber, which is well-staffed by certified operators.

Dr. Yano's Belau Medical Clinic near Ben Franklin in Koror is the best to go for non-emergency care. Dr. Yano is Palauan and has seen just about every tropical ailment imaginable.

## Medical Contacts

**Belau National Hospital & Recompression Chamber**
Ngerekebesang Island
☎ 680-488 2558

**Dr. Yano's Belau Medical Clinic**
Koror center
☎ 680-488-2688

**SDA Clinic**
behind the post office in Koror
☎ 680-488-1911

# Palau Map Index

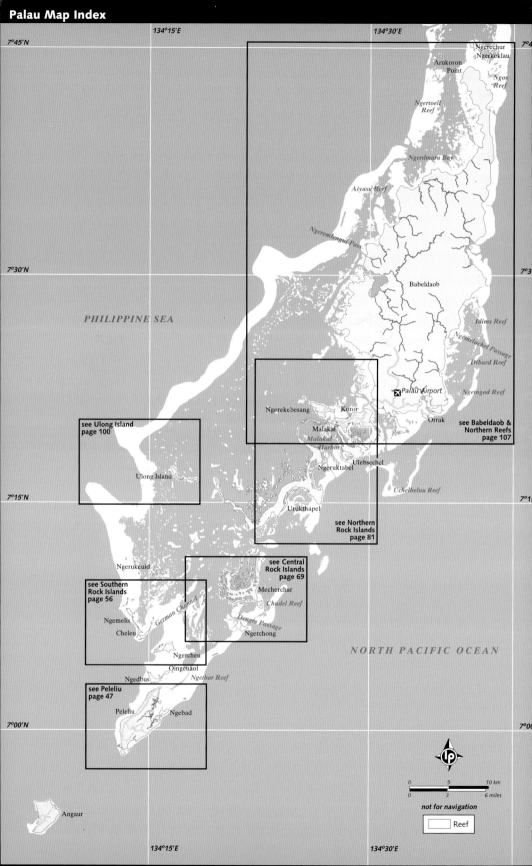

PHILIPPINE SEA

7°45'N
134°15'E
134°30'E

Ngerechur
Ngerkeklau
Arukoron
Point
Ngos
Reef

Ngertoell
Reef

Ngerdmaru Bay

Aiyasu Reef

Ngeremlengui Pass

7°30'N
Babeldaob

Idims Reef

Ngemelachel Passage

Dibard Reef

Palau Airport
Ngemgod Reef

**see Ulong Island
page 100**

Ngerekebesang    Koror
Orrak
**see Babeldaob &
Northern Reefs
page 107**

Malakal
Malakal
Harbor

Ulong Island
Ngeruktabel    Ulebsechel
Ngeruktabel

7°15'N
Uchelbeluu Reef

Urukthapel
**see Northern
Rock Islands
page 81**

Ngerukeuid
**see Central
Rock Islands
page 69**

**see Southern
Rock Islands
page 56**
Mecherchar

Chudel Reef

Ngemelis
Denges Passage

Cheleu
German Channel
Ngerchong

Ngercheu
**NORTH PACIFIC OCEAN**

Oingeuaol

Ngedbus
Ngetbar Reef

**see Peleliu
page 47**

Peleliu    Ngebad

7°00'N

0         5         10 km
0       3       6 miles

*not for navigation*

Angaur

|  | Reef |

# Diving in Palau

Diving in Palau is an experiment in high adventure. The isolated, island-studded archipelago has some of the world's finest wall diving. Deep drop-offs plunge into the rich Indo-Pacific sea. Currents carry divers effortlessly past big fish shoals, schooling sharks and abundant marine life on the coral-covered reeftops. Few places in the world have such a breathtaking undersea terrain combined with tranquil natural beauty on the surface.

The real bonus is that diving here means more than steep walls and exciting drift dives. You can explore history while diving a fleet of coral-encrusted WWII ship and plane wrecks, marvel at more than 1,500 species of fish, and explore the lush inner reefs.

The majority of the diving is done on the southern drop-offs around Ngemelis Island and German Channel. Here, at big-name sites like Big Drop-Off and Blue Corner, you usually drift with the current along sheer walls, taking refuge in the corners to watch marine life. Channels and passes are especially jumping with fish life at tide change. The currents aren't unmanageable, but using a reef hook to hold you in place will help conserve energy and air.

## Reef Hooks

The reef hook, a popular Palau piece of equipment that allows divers to hook into a crevice, slightly inflate to positive buoyancy and float effortlessly against the current, helps if you want to stop and watch the fish action. Most dive shops in Palau sell them and they are beneficial for conserving air and protecting the reef.

Exciting current dives also abound around the Peleliu island tip, where the Pacific Ocean converges with the Philippine Sea. You'll have an excellent chance of seeing spinner dolphins and pelagic fish that usually hang out in deep-blue water.

Wreck diving is done mostly in the mushroom-shaped Rock Islands, where the fringing reef keeps the lagoon free from the weather exposure of the outer reefs. The Rock Islands are also home to numerous marine lakes, including the famous Jellyfish Lake, where you can snorkel with thousands of non-stinging jellies. Accessible dives around Koror include Chandelier Cave, where underwater chambers lead to limestone caves decorated by hanging stalactites, and to wrecks such as the *Iro* and *Gozan Maru*. The outer reef past Ulong Island is home to the Siaes massive underwater tunnel, where black coral blooms and sharks come to rest.

Remote sites on Babeldaob and reefs to the north offer more wrecks, unique log entries and many untouched reefs. You'd be hard-pressed to find anywhere as pristine and beautiful as the Kayangel Atoll, where the long boat journey is well worth the trip.

Almost all dives in Palau are boat dives. Only a few sites around Koror are accessible from shore. Boat operators run daily trips out of Koror, and boats range from high-powered speed boats to luxury live-aboards. You should plan on being gone most of the day, and you'll likely have lunch and a rest on a Rock Island white-sand beach.

# Snorkeling

Palau's reefs provide snorkelers with one of the most diverse, fascinating and beautiful venues in the world. The shallow ledges near the popular drop-offs are good for viewing fish, coral and even pelagics. At sites like Big Drop-Off (Ngemelis Wall), snorkelers can swim along above the divers and share the experience. Snorkeling is also a popular between-dives activity, and local guides can take you to numerous protected coral gardens where the hard corals and fish life will keep you engrossed for hours.

A snorkeler hovers over the sheer drop at Ngemelis.

One site popular snorkeling with visitors worldwide, including some who can't even swim, is Jellyfish Lake, a marine lake on Mecherchar Island. Here a concentration of millions of non-stinging jellyfish have become a real tourist attraction. It is quite a sight to see, especially as they follow the sun in great numbers in search of nutrition. Snorkelers say it is like swimming through gelatin.

At the time of this writing, the population of mastigias jellyfish in Jellyfish Lake was still recovering from a die-off attributed to El Niño. Thus, the numbers are not nearly as great as they have been in the past. But blooms are common and are predicted by scientists. The only question is when this will happen. Ask your guide if the jellies are back in great numbers. The lake also gives snorkelers a great look at the eerie world of a marine lake, even if the jellies aren't there in droves.

# Drift Diving

Drift diving is an integral part of Palau diving, as the tide range average is about 5ft, but can be as great as 7ft. With the volume of water flowing in and out of the channels, across the reefs and along the walls, the current becomes a great buddy, helping propel you through the water with amazing ease. This saves on air and physical energy, and gives you an incredible sensation of flying. It is a good way to go, especially if you're not taking pictures.

If you are, preset your camera and look ahead for your subject, so you can shoot it when it comes into range. Trying to grab on to something while struggling to take a photo in a current usually results in two things: a bad picture and some broken coral, so look and think ahead.

On the walls, there can be up-and-down currents to complicate your drifting. Keep and eye on your computer and a hand on your buoyancy button to compensate. The best bet is to stick with your Palauan dive guide. These guides are among the best drift and wall divers in the world and will keep you out of trouble so you can enjoy the free ride.

# Diving Permits

Rock Island "user permits" must be purchased by anyone diving and snorkeling in Palau. Permits can be purchased through the dive shops and tourist agencies and you must carry it while on the dive boat. The cost is $15 and it is valid for one month. The fees are used to clean the beaches, patrol the waters, enforce environmental laws and to set and maintain dive sites moorings.

# Certification

Palau can be enjoyed by every level of diver and snorkeler and instruction is readily available. Whether you want to get your Open Water certification, or you're looking for advanced or specialty training, you'll be able to arrange something in Palau, as many operators run fully-certified PADI facilities. Nitrox and technical diving can be done here, especially on the wrecks and in the caves. IANTD is the most prevalent tech agency in the country.

# Live-Aboards

Palau is serviced by four live-aboard ships (with more always rumored to come) including the *Ocean Hunter Palau, Palau Aggressor,* Peter Hughes *Sun Dancer II* and the Lesson II *Palau Sport.*

The *Ocean Hunter* provides personalized service for up to six divers. It is big enough to visit all the popular sites, but is also small enough to explore the labyrinth of the Rock Islands. The other three live-aboards cater to larger groups with the *Palau Sport* favoring mostly Japanese divers. It doesn't move around but uses chase boats to shuttle divers to sites.

The *Aggressor* and *Sun Dancer* move around frequently, and both do exploratory diving on chartered trips. These operators can also arrange trips to the remote Southwest Islands, to dive Tobi, Sonsorol and Helen Reef.

The *Ocean Hunter* as seen through the famed Rock Island Arch.

All the ships base themselves in the south of the archipelago where the popular drop-offs are easily accessible. The food is extremely good on all of the live-aboards in Palau, with home-cooked snacks often served between dives.

## Dive Site Icons

The symbols at the beginning of each dive site description provide a quick summary of some of the following characteristics present at each site:

 Good snorkeling or free-diving site.

 Remains or partial remains of a wreck can be seen at this site.

 Sheer wall or drop-off.

 Deep dive. Features of this dive occur in water deeper than 90ft (27m).

 Strong currents may be encountered at this site.

 Strong surge (the horizontal movement of water caused by waves) may be encountered at this site.

 Drift dive. Because of strong currents and/or difficulty in anchoring, a drift dive is recommended at this site.

 Beach/shore dive. This site can be accessed from shore.

 Poor visibility. The site often has visibility of less than 40ft (12m).

 Caves are a prominent feature of this site. Only experienced cave divers should explore inner cave areas.

 Marine preserve. Special regulations apply in this area.

# Pisces Rating System for Dives & Divers

The dive sites in this book are rated according to the following system. These are not absolute ratings but apply to divers at a particular time, diving at a particular place. For instance, someone unfamiliar with prevailing conditions might be considered a novice diver at one dive area, but an intermediate diver at another, more familiar location.

The "Depth Range" given for each site refers to the depth the site is usually dived at. A "+" after the maximum depth indicates that the site has potential to go much deeper.

**Novice:** A novice diver should be accompanied by an instructor or divemaster on all dives. A novice diver generally fits the following profile:

◆ basic scuba certification from an internationally recognized certifying agency
◆ dives infrequently (less than one trip a year)
◆ logged fewer than 25 total dives
◆ little or no experience diving in similar waters and conditions
◆ dives no deeper than 60ft (18m)

**Intermediate:** An intermediate diver generally fits the following profile:

◆ may have participated in some form of continuing diver education
◆ logged between 25 and 100 dives
◆ dives no deeper than 130ft (40m)
◆ has been diving within the last six months in similar waters and conditions

**Advanced:** An advanced diver generally fits the following profile:

◆ advanced certification
◆ has been diving for more than two years; logged over 100 dives
◆ has been diving in similar waters and conditions within the last six months

Regardless of skill level, you should be in good physical condition and know your limitations. If you are uncertain as to your own level of expertise, ask the advice of a local dive instructor. He or she is best qualified to assess your abilities based on the prevailing dive conditions at any given site. Ultimately you must decide if you are capable of making a particular dive, depending on your level of training, recent experience and physical condition, as well as water conditions at the site. Remember that water conditions can change at any time, even during a dive.

# Peleliu Dive Sites

Peleliu, located north of Anguar at the southern end of Palau's archipelago, isn't always accessible for diving, but promises high-voltage action when the seas are calm. The scenic island was the site of a three-month WWII battle that resulted in massive casualties for both the Japanese and the U.S. Marines.

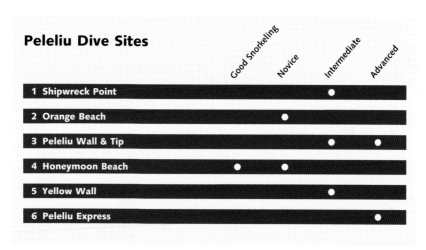

| Peleliu Dive Sites | Good Snorkeling | Novice | Intermediate | Advanced |
|---|:---:|:---:|:---:|:---:|
| 1 Shipwreck Point | | | ● | |
| 2 Orange Beach | | ● | | |
| 3 Peleliu Wall & Tip | | | ● | ● |
| 4 Honeymoon Beach | ● | ● | | |
| 5 Yellow Wall | | | ● | |
| 6 Peleliu Express | | | | ● |

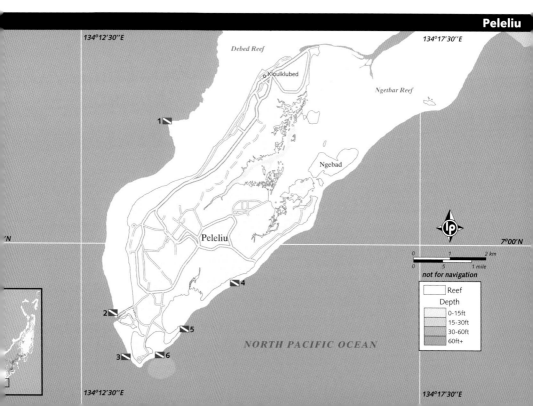

Peleliu

Today, Peleliu is a quiet place with beautiful beaches fringed with ironwood trees and rugged coastlines with rocky outcrops. A high dragonback ridge holds many monuments to those who suffered in the war. Commuter planes fly the 30-minute trip over the enchanting Rock Islands and inter-island ferries and barges make the several-hour trip (depending on weather conditions) to Peleliu. Though a rather long dive boat ride from Koror, and not as popular as the drop-offs just a little to the north, Peleliu's southern tip has gained a glowing reputation as one of the world's finest areas for drift dives. Take an exciting adrenaline current ride on the east side of the island, then swoop along the southwest point, which is always abuzz with marine life.

# 1  Shipwreck Point

Despite its name, Shipwreck Point is not a wreck dive, although the sometimes tricky conditions have caused maritime accidents. It offers good wall diving and a current-fed point that holds a lot of promise for big-fish action. This site is best dived at incoming tide change and is safest when there are no swells

**Location:** Central-west Peleliu

**Depth Range:** 30-120ft (9-36m)

**Access:** Boat

**Expertise Rating:** Intermediate

Spinner dolphins can often be seen off the point.

or (at most) small swells. The reef comes up quickly and it is easy to get caught in the surf, so be careful.

Look for schooling jacks and snapper at the point. The walls, with sea fans and other sessile marine growth, make good photo subjects. In addition to sharks, look out for sailfish and marlin drifting in from the deep. The area is often visited by a pod of spinner dolphins. If they are in a playful mood, they may join the boat and ride in the bow wave as it travels south to Peleliu.

## 2 Orange Beach

Peleliu was a major staging site and the scene of long, bloody battles led by U.S. Marines against the Japanese during WWII. The remnants of this decades-old legacy can still be seen: Orange Beach is littered with amphibious vehicles (known as amtracs), coral encrusted anchors and occasional bomb craters.

**Location:** Southwest Peleliu

**Depth Range:** 40-60ft (12-18m)

**Access:** Boat

**Expertise Rating:** Novice

This makes a nice second dive, combining war artifacts with rich reef life. Currents run along the shallow reeftop, so dives here are usually done as easy drift dives. All kinds of schooling fish gather around the large coral heads, including various types of fusiliers. In the deeper reaches, look for large batfish schools. You'll likely see groupers and titan triggerfish along the bottom. Whitetip reef sharks course the reef looking for small prey.

The bottom slopes into deeper water, so keep an eye on the deep blue for surprises, such as roaming leopard sharks. Sea turtles are also common here and may be seen resting under a coral shelf or lazily looking for a snack.

A hawksbill sea turtle rests near some sea whips.

## 3 Peleliu Wall & Tip

If you want to experience sensory overload, dive Peleliu's southern tip, where the richness of Palau's waters is truly evident. Currents from both sides of this huge archipelago converge here in this wild, open ocean.

**Location:** South of Peleliu

**Depth Range:** 20-130ft (6-40m)

**Access:** Boat

**Expertise Rating:** Intermediate to advanced

The terrain changes around the point, plunging abruptly to at least 900ft. A shallow shelf at 10 to 15ft extends from the shore, but it ends quickly at a coral-covered wall that is alive with marine life. Sharks are often seen along this wall. There are also turtles, sea snakes, large groupers and schools of bumphead parrotfish.

Huge colorful gorgonians grow in as little as 25ft and extend to the depths, increasing in size as you go deeper. You'll occasionally see feathery black coral trees with thick bases and soft corals with royal purple polyps adorning the outcrops. You can explore cuts and crevices painted with encrusting sponges and tunicate colonies. White sea cucumbers comb the brown barrel sponges.

This entire wall is best dived by dropping in far from Peleliu Tip and then drifting to it. The current increases as you approach the tip. A reef hook is advised here, so you can finish the dive by watching the pelagic action, which often includes marlin and occasional tiger sharks.

If you venture past the tip, the reef quickly gets deeper, becoming a long, deepwater finger, and coral cover disappears. This is called **Peleliu Express** (see site #6), where divers like to ride the currents and see what passes by in blue water. This is for advanced divers only. If you aren't comfortable with strong currents and blue water decompression, swim to the shallow area behind the Peleliu Tip where the water eddies and is calm, inflate your safety sausage and wait for the boat to pick you up.

One note of caution: remember you are diving where two ocean currents meet. This is a place to be vigilant about both time and depth. As you approach the tip, the up-current can cause you to ascend 40ft in a matter of seconds, and take you down just as quickly. The current at the surface is also swift at times. Listen carefully to your guide's briefing and do what he or she recommends to ensure the boat picks you up in a timely manner and in safe waters. Carry a signaling device to make sure your boat driver knows when you are up. With these few things in mind, you can enjoy the exciting dive.

Cotton-candy corals blooming along the sheer wall.

Tunicates growing on a red sea fan.

## 4 Honeymoon Beach

A scenic cove and beach on Peleliu's southeast side, this is a nice dive for anyone wanting to see a good mix of coral and invertebrate life. You can either dive shallow or quite deep, but a leisurely dive at 60ft will produce the best results. The reef has several fingers that jut out into the sea. Coral growth on the reeftop is quite competitive. You'll also find arches and over-hangs adorned with soft coral, which make great photo subjects.

Keep an eye out for invertebrate life, includ-ing a nice variety of crinoids and sea stars. At night, look for basket stars coming out of the cracks to feed in the currents.

**Location:** East Peleliu

**Depth Range:** 20-90ft (6-27m)

**Access:** Boat

**Expertise Rating:** Novice

KEVIN DAVIDSON

Harlequin shrimp attempt to feed on a linkia sea star.

# 5   Yellow Wall

Aptly named for the thousands of tube-coral polyps that blossom in the flowing current and make the outer reef wall glow in a golden yellow hue, Yellow Wall is a great variety dive. It can be done as a deep drift or a shallower reeftop swim, or can be combined with the Peleliu Express (for the adrenaline divers in the group).

**Location:** Southeast end of Peleliu Island

**Depth Range:** 40-130ft (12-40m)

**Access:** Boat

**Expertise Rating:** Intermediate

To ride the current, which normally moves south, start where the wall drops steeply near Honeymoon Beach. The wall has a number of pockmarks, cuts, arches and overhangs that are all adorned in sea life. One arch in particular is covered with yellow polyps and makes a perfect

The golden polyps of the tube corals give Yellow Wall its name and striking appearance.

backdrop for a model to swim through. Also keep an eye out for the sea turtles that enjoy feeding on the hydroids.

If drifting along with the current is not in your dive plan, swim up top to observe life in the shallow coral gardens. Check out schools of sweetlips, snappers and emperors, and look for eels in the coral heads, and large groupers under the table corals.

## 6  Peleliu Express

Some people swear by this dive and others swear at it. This is because it is a major drift dive, is rather deep and has a current that can take you off the reef and miles out to open sea. This dive is sometimes combined with a Yellow Wall dive, as the two run together. Why do it? For the chance of seeing Mr. Big!

The southern end of Peleliu has a current-swept finger jutting out into the sea.

**Location:** Southeast end of Peleliu

**Depth Range:** 60-130ft (18-40m)

**Access:** Boat

**Expertise Rating:** Advanced

Hook on to the reef along the expressway

KEVIN DAVIDSON

The wild currents off Peleliu's southern tip sometimes bring in pelagic sea life, such as these pilot whales.

and watch for fish action. Large pelagic fish that normally show up here include ocean-going pilot whales, whitetip sharks, grey reefs, bronze whalers, sailfish and marlin. Dogtooth tuna (sometimes in schools), Spanish mackerel and albacore tuna are also seen cruising through.

As this area is beaten by current, the reef does not have a lot of coral growth.

Hardy sea whips bend in the current and the tougher hard corals pop up from the reef base. A safety sausage and good surface conditions are a must before attempting this wild ride in the sea. Decompression is done while floating with the current in the open ocean, as the reef becomes a deepwater finger, leaving no shallow reef for reference.

## Monkey Time at the Farthest Outpost

Though the dive boats shy away from the trip to Anguar, you can take the 55-minute commuter flight (with a brief stopover in Peleliu) from Koror. The ruggedly beautiful little island, home to about 200 people, is great to cruise around on a scooter or bike, which are available to rent from a number of local entrepreneurs. Anguar dive operators can also take you diving at Santa Maria Point along the northeast shore. Overnight home-stays on the quiet island are easily arranged through the Palau Visitors Authority.

Anguar's biggest claim to fame are the wild macaque monkeys. These are feisty descendants of a couple of monkeys brought to the islands in the 1900s to monitor air quality in the phosphate mines. Accidentally released, the crab-eating monkeys proliferated in the lush jungles. Nowadays, the macaques are not in good graces with the local residents, as they occasionally come in from the jungle to steal from back porches, clotheslines and gardens.

There are fantastic blowholes near the mining area coastline. Angaur also has a place called Ngadalog Beach, where legend has it the souls of deceased Palauans go before they pass through to the next world.

# Southern Rock Islands Dive Sites

The entire southern end of the Palau archipelago is blessed with world-class wall diving and this region, including Ngemelis and Turtle Cove, has some of the world's most famous dive sites. Dramatic drop-offs at sites such as the famed Blue Corner and New Drop-Off attract divers and underwater photographers from around the world. Many walls and jutting undersea points are replete with sharks, barracuda schools and just about every other form of marine life.

Most live-aboards base themselves in this area. Land-based divers travel about an hour by high-speed boat to get here from Koror, winding through the Rock Island maze. Divers typically stay here diving all day, lunching and snorkeling on the beaches at Turtle Cove, Big Drop-Off or Two Dogs Island. The islands have interesting bird life and rugged limestone terrain. Be careful as the limestone is razor sharp and can easily cut through your dive booties.

The Ngemelis coral gardens expose at low tide.

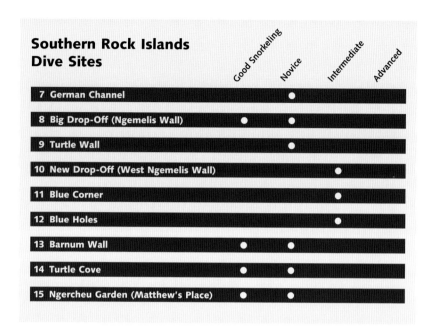

## Southern Rock Islands Dive Sites

| | Good Snorkeling | Novice | Intermediate | Advanced |
|---|:---:|:---:|:---:|:---:|
| 7 German Channel | | ● | | |
| 8 Big Drop-Off (Ngemelis Wall) | ● | ● | | |
| 9 Turtle Wall | | ● | | |
| 10 New Drop-Off (West Ngemelis Wall) | | | ● | |
| 11 Blue Corner | | | ● | |
| 12 Blue Holes | | | ● | |
| 13 Barnum Wall | ● | ● | | |
| 14 Turtle Cove | ● | ● | | |
| 15 Ngercheu Garden (Matthew's Place) | ● | ● | | |

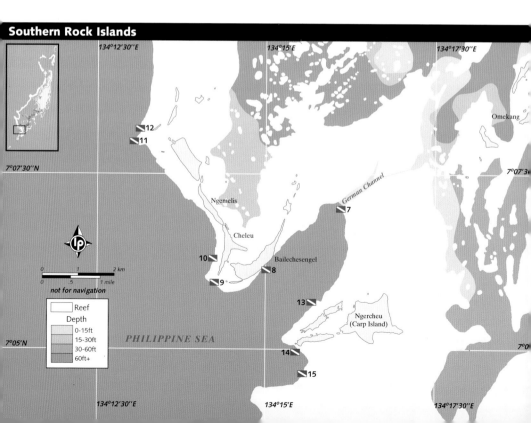

## Southern Rock Islands

# 7    German Channel

**Location:** North of Ngemelis Wall

**Depth Range:** 20-120ft (6-40m)

**Access:** Boat

**Expertise Rating:** Novice

Heading south to the Ngemelis Wall as you motor down from Koror, you pass an area of broad sand flats 10 to 40ft underwater. The reflection from the white sand turns the sea a bright shade of turquoise. This vast expanse—where the Germans blasted through the reef to ease boat passage during their 1899-1914 Palau occupation—was not dived for sport until a few years ago. The channel itself is quite shallow, but the coral gardens around it are deeper and beautifully manicured by nature.

It now has a number of buoys marking deeper areas and is heavily dived. It is a main passageway for boats, so divers should not surface too quickly and should always signal their presence with a safety sausage.

Palau's tide range can be as much as 7ft, which means the water funneling over these flats reaches a respectable but not treacherous speed. Divers merely have to drop over the edge of the boat and go with the flow.

The odd juvenile barramundi cod also hovers over the corals and observant divers can usually spot a cuttlefish in these thickets. Cuttlefish resemble large squid. They are curious by nature, and will watch divers and react by flashing various hues of electric color. Large triggerfish travel the flats, turtles sleep under

# The Language of Color and Love

Cuttlefish, octopus and squid can change color at will. These unique reef critters, members of the cephalopod class, live in water ranging from 20 to 40ft and in literally the blink of an eye they can adapt their camouflage. They do this for protection but also when they are curious, amorous, alarmed or showing aggression. Cephalopods, among the most advanced of all invertebrates, can maneuver better than most sea animals. A small jet just below the cuttlefish's tentacles can point in any direction and expels water, allowing the cuttlefish to shoot along, sometimes at blinding speed.

Their three layers of cell structures are known as chromatophores, whose color pigments are controlled by radial muscles in the cuttlefish's unique dual (local and central) nervous system. The cells expand and contract, creating a play of light and color that results in the most amazing light show displayed by any creature on earth. They have the most powerful neurological system known to science and their lightning ability to change color and adapt camouflage is unrivaled in the animal world. Cuttlefish tend to be territorial, so once you see one, you can return to the same reef site and likely see it again.

platter corals and sharks frequently pass by. Many areas also have garden eels.

Gorgonian fans with scarlet skeletons and snowy, white polyps quiver, extending into the current. Crinoids of many hues abound on top of coral heads. Forests of staghorn corals provide protection for clouds of damselfish.

Big mantas are known to feed in formation at tide change near the mouth of the channel. You'll find a manta cleaning station near the drop-off—just sit on the bottom and wait for them to come. They feed above this area, so look up into the shallow water, as there may be action above your head.

A manta feeding in the Channel.

## 8   Big Drop-Off (Ngemelis Wall)

One of the best-known wall dives in sport diving is the Big Drop-Off. Also called Ngemelis Wall , this sheer cut supports just about every form of marine life you can imagine. Located just south of the historic German Channel, the drop-off starts in extremely shallow water (sometimes knee deep at low tide) and falls to depths greater than 900ft.

**Location:** Ngemelis west channel

**Depth Range:** 3-130ft (1-40m)

**Access:** Boat

**Expertise Rating:** Novice

The feeling you get after kicking away from the shallow reeftop and buoyantly hanging over the inky abyss is similar to a sky diver's rush.

A gentle current runs along the southeastern wall, which is the most frequently dived area. You can dump the air from your BC and free-float to just about any depth desired while experiencing a casual drift dive that makes swimming optional.

Sea fans are abundant along the wall, getting larger the deeper you go. Crinoids, looking like holiday tinsel, sit on these fans while feeding in the current. The wall is also home to great barrel sponges and pretzel-like rope sponge formations.

The fish population is also quite varied. A large resident Napoleon wrasse makes the wall home, and schools of sergeant majors and yellowtail course vertically, seemingly spilling into the water from above the reef. Also look for schools of parrotfish and an abundance of pyramid butterflyfish. The crevices hold leaf fish and fire dartfish. This is also a great night dive with the tubastrea corals blossoming into fields of golden polyps.

The top of the wall is rich in marine life with many sea anemones and clouds of chromis and small reef fish. For sheer beauty and plenty of fish life, Palau's Big Drop-Off is hard to rival.

A swimmer frolics with the fish at the Ngemelis swimming hole.

# 9 Turtle Wall

This site, found between the more-famous Big Drop-Off and New Drop-Off, is a popular gathering site for green and hawksbill sea turtles. The buoy marking the site displays its other moniker, Fern's Wall, so-named after a popular local dive guide. In addition to the turtles, this site is known for abundant soft corals and gorgonian sea fans.

This is a drift dive that can run either east or west, depending on the direction of the currents at a particular time. Tubastrea and small hard corals adorn the wall. Deeper sea fans, soft coral colonies and crimson sea whips are even more spectacular.

**Location:** Ngemelis west channel

**Depth Range:** 15-130ft (4.5-40m)

**Access:** Boat

**Expertise Rating:** Novice

Currents flowing from Big Drop-Off carry lots of nutrients. Expect to see schools of rainbow runners, grey reef and whitetip sharks, fusiliers and Napoleon wrasse. Larger animals can be observed farther out. You may see mantas feeding and even an occasional whale shark.

A green sea turtle cruises the wall.

## 10 New Drop-Off (West Ngemelis Wall)

The name may not be the catchiest, but that doesn't detract from the excitement of the marine life here. Blue Corner has long been Palau's hottest drop-off attraction, but New Drop-Off, full of shark and barracuda action, is a close rival for this designation. The site also features Napoleon wrasse, sea turtles and eagle rays.

**Location:** Southwest tip, Ngemelis Island

**Depth Range:** 20-120ft (6-36m)

**Access:** Boat

**Expertise Rating:** Intermediate

Sometimes referred to as West Ngemelis Wall, this site is right around the corner from Turtle Wall, near a snorkeling area called **Fairyland**, where the nice array of hard corals, crevices and small invertebrates is good for macro-photography.

The steep drop-off starts between 15 to 30ft, depending where you jump in. This area has intense current, and keeping yourself neutral can be a little unnerving when side currents, down currents and up currents are all bouncing you around—you feel a little like a cork. Once you get a handle on what is going on, you'll to appreciate the area, which is alive with fish.

Schools of bluestripe snappers and larger grey snappers swim along the drop-off. Both sharpnose and blackbar barracuda are frequent visitors. Currents

A diver photographs bluestripe snappers at New Drop-Off.

propel divers around many cuts and corners, and it's not unusual to go sweeping around a corner only to find yourself within a few feet of silvery barracuda hovering near the wall. A reef hook helps if you want to stop and watch the fish action. Most dive shops in Palau sell them and they are beneficial to conserving air and protecting the reef.

New Drop-Off has its share of beautiful coral fans and soft corals as well. The wall is alive with small tropicals, and sea anemones are found along the upper reaches. Visibility is about 80ft along this wall but the tidal flow exits the inner reef flats leaving the water a little murky. New Drop-Off is one of the bottomless dives that has made Palau famous, so it is wise to keep a good eye on your depth gauge and pay attention to what you're doing. It is easy to get distracted swimming with a turtle or some other fascinating marine animal here, but you must be careful or you'll completely botch your dive profile.

## 11 Blue Corner

Blue Corner off Ngemelis Island consistently sizzles with electric fish action. Large sharks are common, as are small sharks, sea turtles, groupers, schools of barracuda, snappers, small tropicals, Napoleon wrasse, bumphead parrotfish and even an occasional moray eel or sea snake. Incredibly big stingrays have also been seen here. The critter list is almost endless.

The Corner is a flat area of the reef starting at about 45ft and running for a couple hundred yards out into the sea before dropping off abruptly. Small hills, sand tunnels and gorges cut into the reef flat. A strong tidal current runs

**Location:** Southwest reef, Ngemelis Island

**Depth Range:** 40-130ft (12-40m)

**Access:** Boat

**Expertise Rating:** Intermediate

through, providing food for the little guys at the bottom of the food chain, who, in turn, attract middle- and upper-chain critters.

Start a typical dive by descending along the wall through schooling fish and at least a dozen reef sharks that are curious about you and perhaps alerted to your presence by your bubbles. Before the tip, a cut in the wall boasts immense gorgonian sea fans and feathery black coral trees.

At about 50ft, hang out and watch the schools of fish coursing around the corner. Some fish schools actually mix together, with as many as four different species swimming in one dense formation. Use a reef hook to remain stationary in the current. It will help you avoid

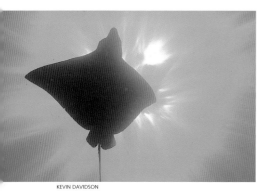
KEVIN DAVIDSON
An eagle ray cruises over in crystal clear water.

damaging the coral, and makes it easier to watch the action. Look a little farther into the heavier coral growth to see as many as a half-dozen hawksbill turtles grazing on hydroids.

The sharks here are well fed naturally, but treat them with respect anyway, especially during mating season (May and June), when they tend to get more aggressive. During this time schools of Moorish idols also swim along the wall. Sharks will actually herd them to the surface to feed upon them. The deeper reaches of Blue Corner harbor a large school of horse-eye jacks. Bigger pelagics include hammerhead and tiger sharks, marlin, sailfish and even schooling yellowfin tuna.

Because it is so consistently active, Blue Corner is a mecca for world-class underwater photographers, and should be considered a must for every serious diver. Be warned that there can be many boats and divers here during high season. The currents can be powerful and tricky at times, sweeping ascending divers right off the point. Be sure to watch for down and up currents running along the walls. For these reasons, always dive with a safety sausage.

The famous Blue Corner juts into the open sea and then drops to the depths.

## 12 Blue Holes

The Blue Holes are four vertical shafts that open on top of the reef flat near Blue Corner. The shafts lead to the outer reef wall. It is popular to dive through the Blue Holes and continue to the Blue Corner.

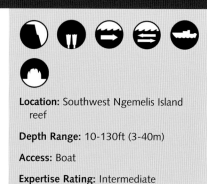

**Location:** Southwest Ngemelis Island reef

**Depth Range:** 10-130ft (3-40m)

**Access:** Boat

**Expertise Rating:** Intermediate

As you descend and drift down the shafts, watch the refracted sunlight dance through the water and play with the blue hues. Tubastrea and wire corals adorn the hole walls. Black coral grows near the bottom exit. These corals don't need the direct sunlight other corals require.

The dive is quite deep, with the first exit at about 85ft, where the water gets darker. Incredibly large fish live here, including immense wahoos and ocean-going tuna.

Spotted leopard nurse sharks are known to rest along the sandy bottom. They'll allow divers close approach before being coaxed from their resting spot.

Sharks with zebra stripes are juvenile leopards whose stripes will eventually become spots. Whitetip sharks sleep here as well.

When the current is right, divers can exit the shafts and drift all the way to Blue Corner, watching for sharks and turtles on the way. Another alternative is to ascend and explore the outer wall, which has gorgonian sea fans and rich violet soft corals.

Divers exit to the outer wall from the Blue Holes cavern.

There is a cave at one end of the bottom of the holes called **The Temple of Doom** which is pitch black with only one exit. Venturing into this area is for extremely experienced cave-trained divers only, and should not be entered without proper planning, lights, a guide and back-up air.

## 13 Barnum Wall

Though just a short ride across the channel from the popular Big Drop-Off, Barnum Wall is one of the least known dives in the area.

Divers follow a sloping decline whose relief areas are full of corals. Big cracks and crevices provide homes for a number of marine critters, such as large groupers and sweetlips. Smaller reef fish like pyramid butterflies and schools of fusiliers are also common. You may even find turtles resting near the large platter corals.

The wall has sea fans (though smaller that those at Ngemelis Wall) and large stands of leather corals with soft, swaying tentacles that make them resemble anemones. Barnum starts shallow, in about 10ft. Crinoids, in many hues, from brilliant combinations of evergreen to gold and black, proliferate on the reeftop.

**Location:** Across from Big Drop-Off (Ngemelis Wall)

**Depth Range:** 10-130ft (3-40m)

**Access:** Boat

**Expertise Rating:** Novice

KEVIN DAVIDSON
A wire coral shrimp is well camouflaged at Barnum Wall.

## 14 Turtle Cove

Turtle Cove is a popular rest stop for Blue Corner divers. The cove has a shaded beach and good snorkeling. The cove has two buoys: one is near the cove's blue hole and the other, farther east, usually has an immense school of striped snapper and goatfish swirling in a bright yellow ball near its anchor point. This school is great for snorkelers and for photographers looking to take nice fish pictures.

**Location:** North of Peleliu

**Depth Range:** 5-130ft (1.5-40m)

**Access:** Boat

**Expertise Rating:** Novice

The blue hole sits atop the shallow reef flat. At low tide, it is possible to stand at the edge of the hole with part of your body out of the water. Underwater, as you drift through hole, you'll see red and yellow soft coral trees in about 30ft. The soft corals used to be more abundant, but careless divers falling and over-kicking have destroyed many of these delicate animals. This marine environment is fragile—pay special attention to buoyancy control.

The inside of the hole is honeycombed with exits at various depths. One small passage at 35ft is home to a large lionfish family. It has lived in this little cave for years and is occasionally joined by a grouper. A little farther down, a large window opens to the outer wall at 70ft. All along this area are elegant, golden sea fans and wispy black coral trees. A leopard nurse shark sometimes sleeps on the bottom, which slopes down to about 90ft, then falls off to more than 200ft.

The outer wall rises nearly to the surface on both sides and ends at a point. Flowing crinoids adorn burgundy and cream sea fans. Fluted oysters display their kaleidoscopic mantles until scared shut by a burst of bubbles. Fusiliers and tiger-striped sweetlips add to the fish action. Grey reef sharks and fish schools are found at the point during incoming tide. Also, keep a lookout for Titan triggerfish nests.

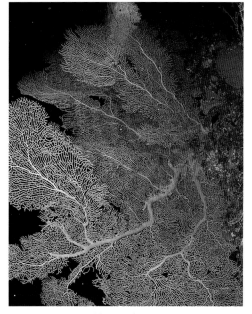

A giant golden sea fan greets divers at 70ft.

Resident snappers and goatfish splash the upper reef with brilliant color.

# 15 Ngercheu Garden (Matthew's Place)

This wonderfully protected cove with little current is great for a casual dive. The cove's gentle incline allows you to explore anywhere between 20 to 80ft. It's named for pioneer Palauan diver Matthew Elebelau, as this was his favorite spot to find resting turtles and colorful tropical fish. Castle, branching and table corals all share space on this healthy hard-coral reef.

**Location:** South of Turtle Cove

**Depth Range:** 20-80ft (6-24m)

**Access:** Boat

**Expertise Rating:** Novice

Matthew's Place is a great site to poke around looking for unusual critters, especially at night. Some of the amazing night sightings include a slumbering giant Napoleon wrasse with a cadre of cleaner shrimp scouring its face, and the elusive and comical firefish. The firefish is a member of the lionfish family, but scurries across the reef floor, as opposed to the fluid swimming motion of its larger cousin. Watch for shells, shrimp and sleeping parrotfish.

In 1999, fish expert K.C. Miller found a very unusual critter not normally seen in Palau waters. It was a very small lacey scorpionfish (about 2 to 3 inches long) in about 40 to 50ft. The rare little fish was perfectly camouflaged, sitting on dead coral and blending in with a stringy pink algae. Test your fish-finding skills by trying to find this one again.

The brilliant and nocturnal firefish is common at Matthew's Place.

# Central Rock Islands Dive Sites

Nestled in the Rock Islands are many nice channel dives, marine lakes and arches and tunnels. Some of the premier novelty attractions are found here, such as lakes filled with non-stinging jellyfish and beds of giant clams. There are also some wonderful current dives in the inside channels. Sites inside the Rock Islands are almost always accessible and the outer reefs are a convenient boat ride away and aren't heavily dived.

## Palau's Marine Lakes

Palau's Rock Islands are home to over 50 marine lakes, more than anywhere else in the world. Each lake has its own unique ecosystem and unusual creatures that thrive in it.

Five Palauan marine lakes have significant numbers of jellyfish, such as Jellyfish Lake (see site #17) on Mecherchar Island. During the day as the jellies follow the sun, they concentrate in great numbers. The sensation is otherworldly as thousands of pulsing aliens surge to soak up the sun.

Others have creatures that have adapted in other ways. Flatworm Lake is full of millions of marine flatworms. Clear shrimp live in Shrimp Lake as do stinging *Cassiopea* jellyfish. Cavern Lake features stinging sponges. Ketau Lake is a giant with full-grown reef sharks. A bizarre horned sea cucumber lives in Tee Lake.

The marine lakes are protected marine preserves and a licensed guide must accompany visitors. Most are not easily accessible (you'll need to don your hiking boots), and some are closed to the public. Contact the Palau Visitors Authority or Planet Blue kayaking tours to see which lakes are currently being accessed.

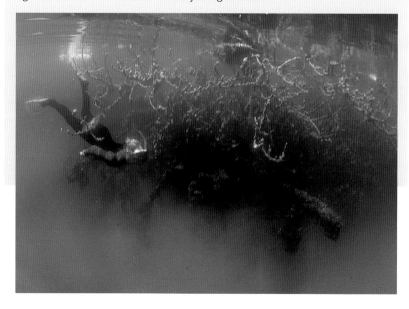

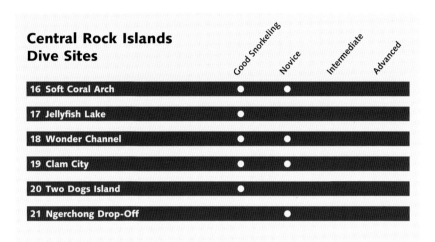

## Central Rock Islands Dive Sites

| | Good Snorkeling | Novice | Intermediate | Advanced |
|---|---|---|---|---|
| **16 Soft Coral Arch** | ● | ● | | |
| **17 Jellyfish Lake** | ● | | | |
| **18 Wonder Channel** | ● | ● | | |
| **19 Clam City** | ● | ● | | |
| **20 Two Dogs Island** | ● | | | |
| **21 Ngerchong Drop-Off** | | ● | | |

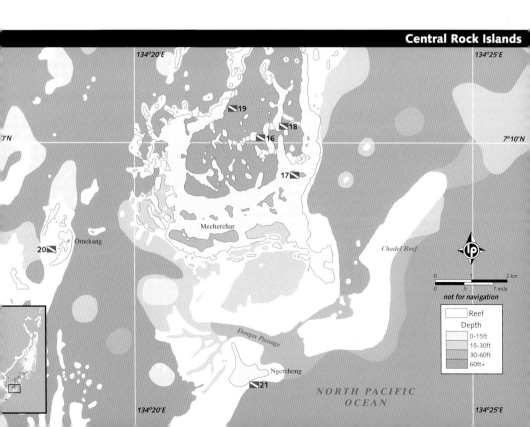

**Central Rock Islands**

134°20'E  134°25'E

7°10'N

19

18

16

17

Mecherchar

Omekang

20

Chudel Reef

0        1        2 km
0        .5        1 mile
*not for navigation*

Reef
Depth
0-15ft
15-30ft
30-60ft
60ft+

*Denges Passage*

Ngerchong

21

NORTH PACIFIC
OCEAN

134°20'E  134°25'E

## 16 Soft Coral Arch

Primarily a snorkeling site, Soft Coral Arch is one of the few places in the Rock Islands where huge soft corals grow in assorted shades, from vibrant reds to soft pastels, painting the seafloor like multi-colored cotton candy.

**Location:** North of Mecherchar

**Depth:** 15ft (4.5m)

**Access:** Boat

**Expertise Rating:** Novice

These corals, which feed on nutrients carried by the current that flows through the arched gap, are best accessed while snorkeling. They are extremely delicate and can be easily damaged or even killed by fin kick or other inadvertent contact, so be very careful. A resident school of yellowtail fusiliers will surround you when you don your snorkel and jump from the boat into the water.

Unlike many other Rock Island sites, Soft Coral Arch is not a marine lake, so does not require the extra effort to access. This is just an easy, colorful snorkeling site.

Yellowtail fusiliers swarm divers at the mouth of the arch.

## 17 Jellyfish Lake

Since *National Geographic* magazine published an article in the early '80s on Palau's marine lakes, Jellyfish Lake has become a popular snorkeling destination. This is one of the few places in the world where you can swim surrounded by jellyfish without the risk of being stung.

**Location:** Mecherchar Island

**Depth Range:** 0-30ft (0-9m)

**Access:** Hike with a local guide to marine lake

**Expertise Rating:** Snorkeling only

At this site, the jellyfish normally number in the hundreds of thousands but there have been fluctuations attributed to weather phenomena, such as El Niño. The 1997-98 El Niño led to a rapid die-off, causing the mastigias jellyfish—one of the two jellyfish species here—population to plummet. However, it seems time, stable weather conditions and lack of predators allow the population to once again flourish.

This is primarily a snorkeling site, as only the upper reaches of the lake—where freshwater and saltwater mix—are safe to dive. Below 50ft, divers would find a bacterial layer that is like swimming through a black wall. Below this, where the sun is virtually blocked out, is deoxygenated water containing highly toxic concentrations of hydrogen sulfide. This can cause long-term respiratory problems. Exposure of even a couple of minutes is dangerous, so diving here is not recommended.

You'll start this adventure by motoring around nearly exposed coral patches to a shaded jungle cove found deep in the islands. The cove contains giant tridacna clams that can be easily seen while snorkeling. A Faulkner razor coral, named after its discoverer Douglas Faulkner, is also abundant here.

To get to the lake, you need to hike from the cove through the rocky limestone forest. Wear appropriate footwear, such as sport or hiking shoes. You'll hike up a steep hill to the top of Mecherchar, then down to the edge of a briny swamp.

Snorkel slowly and cautiously through the swamp so you don't run into the rocks, which are difficult to see. The water soon clears up and drops to a depth of about 10ft. Below, decaying vegetation mixes with a maze of roots. Small black-belted cardinalfish dart in and out. A closer look at the roots reveals small, white anemones with flowing tentacles. The anemones, which feed on juvenile jellyfish, are the jellyfish's only enemy.

The two types of jellyfish found here are mastigias and moon jellies. Most prominent is the mastigias species, which, in their isolation from predators over the millennia, have lost both their ability and need to sting. Instead, they have developed a symbiotic relationship with

Snorkeling with the non-stinging jellies feels like swimming through gelatin.

Tiny anemones prey on unsuspecting jellies in Jellyfish Lake.

algae, called zooxanthellae, inside their bodies. The algae get energy from the sun, and the jellyfish in turn get energy from the algae.

You'll find the heaviest concentrations of jellyfish in areas that get the most direct sunlight. As the sun moves across the lake in the afternoon, the jellyfish group together and move with it. Snorkelers can expect to be surrounded on all sides by hundreds of thousands of the animals. Diving down into this sea of pulsing, gelatinous umbrellas and looking up at the sun is nothing short of surreal.

The lake also gives the snorkeler the rare chance to experience a marine lake even if the jellies aren't plentiful.

A word of caution. Though you won't get stung by a jellyfish, be aware that voracious saltwater crocodiles live in the Rock Islands. Ask your guide if any have been spotted recently in Jellyfish Lake before hopping in.

## 18 Wonder Channel

Wonder Channel, in the heart of the Rock Islands, provides a scenic drift dive along a sloping wall that is loaded with a variety of coral, fish and invertebrates. Numerous sea fans, crinoids, sponges and other filter-feeding animals thrive here because of the abundant food source flowing through the channel.

Don't expect great visibility in these nutrient-filled waters, though it never drops below 30ft. This dive is a carnival ride through a true coral wonderland. The channel is normally dived during tide change, which can vary as much as 7ft in Palau. This great flux and flow of water provides a swift current, making

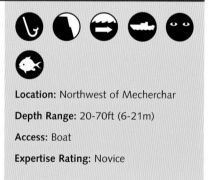

**Location:** Northwest of Mecherchar

**Depth Range:** 20-70ft (6-21m)

**Access:** Boat

**Expertise Rating:** Novice

diving effortless. You can usually feel the tug of the current as soon as you ease over the side of the boat. Just drop down, become neutral and float along for the ride. If something interesting comes

The islands near the channel are good for snorkeling, but drift diving is the norm in deeper waters.

along, tuck behind coral cover along the slope to get out of the current.

Staghorn and elkhorn corals dominate at the top of the channel. Clouds of silver and turquoise chromis find a haven in these branching formations. Deeper down, sea fans and wispy black coral trees abound. Small hawkfish and pipefish weave through the lacework of the gorgonians, and crinoids perch on their edges. Schools of yellowtail seem to swoop down from above, often curiously encircling divers. Sea anemones and smaller invertebrates are also good for macrophotographers. Sponge formations resemble everything from Greek vases to rope sculptures. Small fish, not yet bait size, often seek shelter in the sponges. Add to this an occasional giant tridacna or green moray eel and it is easy to see why Wonder Channel is so popular.

## Bone Caves

Near the pass to Mecherchar is *Yii ra Beldokel*, which, loosely translated, means Cave of the Dead. In the ancient days, the people who inhabited this area would bring their dead to this cave, laying the bodies, which were wrapped in woven mats, inside. It is believed

these people later moved on to inhabit the far-away southern islands of Tobi and Sonsorol, where the present-day language and customs are different from those in northern Palau.

You can visit the cave in between dives. The boat takes you to the tiny sandy shore where the cave mouth meets the beach. You then wade in chest-high water to the cave mouth, inside of which a huge cavern (50 yards wide) opens up and you can walk in for quite a way. The only light spills in from the entrance. Bones can be found along the walls and in the far reaches, where stalactites and stalagmites still form.

If you happen to visit this ancient site, tread lightly as the bones are fragile. Treat this sacred site as Palauans do, with respect.

# 19 Clam City

**Location:** Northwest of Mecherchar

**Depth Range:** 20-30ft (6-9m)

**Access:** Boat

**Expertise Rating:** Novice

There are a couple of places in Palau where you can see giant tridacna clams. One is at the government-run Palau Mariculture Demonstration Center (PMDC) in Koror, but by far the most scenic is Clam City, a private enterprise in the Rock Islands. Here, various species of giant clams have been intentionally placed in sandy offshore areas, allowing them to thrive and spawn. Nearby channels and currents carry the clam larvae out to the east and west reefs, so this is a very functional tourist attraction. Clams at both the PMDC and Clam City are protected by law and cannot be taken.

The giant clams synthesize the solar energy they receive through the tiny black "eyes" on their mantles. If a diver swims by, the receptors will sense the lack of light and close, sometimes rapidly. The mantle colors range from brilliant green and vibrant blues, to more subdued earth tones in tans and brown. Look for small fish and crabs near the clams for interesting macrophotographic compositions.

The giant tridacnas thrive in shallow water where sunlight aids their feeding.

## Giant Clams

Palau's giant tridacna clams regularly grow more than 4ft (1.2m) in length and can weigh more than 500 pounds (230kg), making them the world's largest bivalve mollusk. Their fleshy mantles have intriguingly mottled designs of browns, greens and iridescent blues. Each design is like a fingerprint, formed by the introduction of algae to the clam's mantle. The older clams are no spring chickens—some can live more than a hundred years.

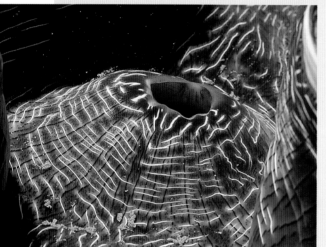

There are seven species of tridacna clams in Palau's waters. Palauans have long eaten the meat of the clams, and grind up the smaller shells for lime powder to chew with betel nut.

The main threat to the clams, however, comes from outside poachers, who are wiping out the tridacna on coral reefs around the Pacific, over-harvesting to a point where few are left for breeding. The poachers often take only the profitable adductor muscle of the clam, which is prized as a delicacy and aphrodisiac in the Orient, while the rest of the clam is left to rot.

## 20    Two Dogs Island

Almost everyone who dives in southern Palau seems to wind up at the uninhabited Two Dogs Island (also known as Little Omekang Island) for lunch or a respite during a day of diving. Named for the two dogs that were left on the island in the 1990s, the site's shallow and sandy seafloor is home to varied marine life.

**Location:** North of German Channel

**Depth Range:** 0-20ft (0-6m)

**Access:** Boat

**Expertise Rating:** Snorkeling only

The sandy seafloor holds much for the snorkeler to see, including sea stars, sand blennies and tridacna clams. Milkfish and other shallow-water schooling fish move through here as well. Take care not to snorkel too far out into the boat lane. Captains are careful, but there have been accidents here.

The work of the waves and the gnawing of the iron-toothed chiton on the island's undercut edges help demonstrate how the mushroom-shaped Rock Islands were formed. This prehistoric-looking chiton hangs out just below the waterline.

On land at Two Dogs Island, small, natural limestone caves formerly used by Japanese soldiers are within hiking distance from shore. The hike takes you over jagged limestone and along a narrow ridge. At a couple of points the ridge falls into an unforgiving pit, so be careful. Skulls and bones of at least three soldiers were found in one of the farthest caves up the ridge.

The dogs, by the way, are well fed. When tourists can't feed them, they do quite well catching their own fish in the shallows around the island.

The shallows of the "picnic islands" are fun for snorkelers.

## 21 Ngerchong Drop-Off

**Location:** Southeast Ngerchong Island

**Depth Range:** 20-130ft (6-40m)

**Access:** Boat

**Expertise Rating:** Novice

This dive is often saved by dive operators for times when windy or stormy weather closes out the more popular dive sites at Ngemelis and Peleliu. It is a rich and rewarding dive and, for maximum results, should be done at incoming tide.

The dive starts on a sloping reef. You may need to swim with a little energy to get over the reef edge but after that a nice drift takes you along the sculpted slope. The hill is highlighted by table corals and some large gorgonian sea fans. Crannies and crevices are home to lobster, eel and nudibranchs. The water column is rich with schooling fish, including grey reef sharks. A variety of groupers live in the cascading shelves, and pufferfish have even been seen mating at Ngerchong.

The sloping wall eventually leads to the Ngerchong Channel mouth, where the fish life increases dramatically. While drifting along the water column, expect to see mackerel, occasional dogtooth tuna and lots of grey reef sharks that will approach divers quite closely. Manta rays also coast along the deeper reaches while feeding in the currents. The drift into the channel takes you past schools of jacks, black snappers and longnose barracuda. The channel opens up to a shallow shelf that rises to 20ft and is topped with large coral heads. Look for sea turtles and banded sea snakes.

A photographer looks deep into the coral gardens to find anemones and other small marine creatures.

# Northern Rock Islands Dive Sites

While every dive shop makes the daily pilgrimage to the big name sites, you can skip the long boat ride and enjoy some great dives in the northern region of the Rock Islands, around Koror and Ulong Island. Just a short boat ride will take you to sunken WWII shipwrecks, such as the *Amatsu Maru* and *Chuyo Maru*, which now rest at the bottom of the Koror anchorage area. Also explore the popular *Iro Maru*, whose intact bowgun and crosstrees are heavily encrusted with lush marine growth.

The secluded bays and coves around Koror harbor juvenile marine life and some unique and sought after creatures, like the colorful mandarinfish. Even in inclement weather, many of these caves, reefs and passages are protected and accessible, so divers can get their underwater fix even if it is not possible to go to the drop-offs.

The outer reefs around historic Ulong Island are some of Palau's richest and the Ulong Channel (also called Ngerumekaol Channel) is a major spawning ground for many kinds of fish.

A boat on a glassy sea heads through the Rock Island maze.

# Koror Dive Sites

Most divers are based in the Koror area and a number of dive sites close to the town docks hold plenty of beauty and history. A couple of the novelty dives, like the Chandelier Cave, are also part of the area's seascape. While operators save many of these dives for times when weather or big seas close out the big name southern sites, there are some very good dives here. Some folks even go out and do a wreck dive in the mornings, come back to town for lunch, and then head out again in the afternoon for another dive. There are also some very good night dives found in and around Koror.

Historian Klaus Lindemann examines a shipwreck.

## Koror Dive Sites

| | Good Snorkeling | Novice | Intermediate | Advanced |
|---|:---:|:---:|:---:|:---:|
| **22 Short Drop-Off** | ● | ● | | |
| **23 Tim's Reef** | ● | ● | | |
| **24 *Teshio Maru*** | ● | ● | | |
| **25 Jake Floatplane** | ● | ● | | |
| **26 Chandelier Cave** | | | ● | |
| **27 *Ryuko Maru*** | | | ● | |
| **28 *Amatsu Maru*** | | | ● | |
| **29 *Chuyo Maru*** | | | ● | |
| **30 Helmet Wreck** | | ● | | |
| **31 Brown Corner** | ● | ● | | |
| **32 Kesebekuu Channel (Lighthouse)** | | | ● | |
| **33 *Iro Maru*** | ● | ● | | |
| **34 *Gozan Maru*** | | ● | | |

Ryuko Maru

134°25'E

134°30'E

25

Ngerekebesang

Meyuns

26

Ngerchemai

Mekebr

Medalaii

Koror

27  Ryuko Maru

28

31

Amatsu Maru

29

Chuyo Maru

Ngerbached

7°20'N

Malakal

30

Ulebsechel

Ngeruktabel

Ngel Channel

33  Iro Maru

23

32

22

Urukthapel

Uchelbeluu Reef

34  Gozan Maru

7°15'N

0    .5    1    2 km

0    .5    1 mile

not for navigation

Reef

Depth

0-15ft

15-30ft

30-60ft

60ft+

NORTH PACIFIC OCEAN

134°25'E

## 22 Short Drop-Off

This site is so named because it is a short boat ride from Koror, not because the drop-off is shallow. Located near a cut in the outer barrier reef on the archipelago's east side, Short Drop-Off provides a great variety of sea life, especially for macrophotographers, but it can be good for wide-angle photography, too.

**Location:** East-central outer Uchelbeluu Reef

**Depth Range:** 20-130ft (6-40m)

**Access:** Boat

**Expertise Rating:** Novice

Because many divers visiting Palau are hardcore types who want to hit the water the minute they deplane, tour operators can take advantage of the wall and drift diving so conveniently close to Koror's main hotels. It is not uncommon for Short Drop-Off to be a newly arrived diver's first dive, and it's a great way to start a week of diving.

The ride to the reef takes you through the channel and across an open expanse to the reef. During high tide you'll take an alternate route through the Rock Islands, which allows you to experience the greenery and winding waterways.

Once at the site, a quick snorkel reveals an upper reef flat crowded with corals and tons of reef tropicals. Silver chromis abound, as do wrasse, butterflyfish and parrotfish. Colorful encrusting sponges decorate the undersides of many coral heads, painting them in oranges, reds and purples. Tunicate colonies also attach themselves and delicate lace corals fill the rock fissures.

The coral garden gradually slopes down to about 35ft and then drops off abruptly. The wall is sheer in some spots, and a draping sand fall in others. Diving is usually done on the protected inner reef wall, at almost any depth. Sponges and branching corals at 40 to 50ft make a long, exploratory dive quite safe. Look for crocodilefish sitting in ambush in the coral and sand.

Divers will likely encounter hawksbill turtles resting on the ledges or munching on hydroids. Throughout the dive, curious schools of yellowtail fusiliers appear, and look for good reef shark action when the current is running.

The lacy eyelids of the crocodilefish protect it from sunburn.

## Deep-Water Nautilus

Sought after for its beautiful shell with its radial lines and handsome appearance, the chambered nautilus is one of the more unusual creatures found in Pacific waters. It lives in a 15-degree band near the equator. A cephalopod, a sub-family of the mollusk, the nautilus hasn't changed in all of its 400 million years of existence.

Since in Palauan waters the nautilus lives at depths anywhere in the range of 500 to 1,000ft, if you see one while diving, you're down too deep! However, at night nautilus come up as shallow as 200ft to feed. The best way to observe them is to set a basket-style trap in deep water and pull them up, then immediately release them. This is not harmful to the nautilus.

Nautiluses prefer near-freezing water temperatures, but they are quite capable of surviving for several hours in warmer tropical water.

There are several different types of nautiluses, with only some slight variations in the shell or appearance: the *Pompilius* is common and the *Scrobiculaus* is one of the rarest. Palau's indigenous species is called *Belauensis* for Palau's traditional name, "Belau."

*- Kevin Davidson*

## 23 Tim's Reef

Few people make it out to this reef, but it is a marvelous place to dive and snorkel, combining history and a beautiful reef. It is about halfway from Koror to Short Drop-off and features a somewhat circular reef surrounded by a couple of prolific channels. The best dive spot is on the southwest side. In the shallow water on the reeftop, you'll find many small table corals with holes, cracks and small crevices that shelter colorful tropicals.

**Location:** Near Mutremdiu Channel

**Depth Range:** 5-70ft (1.5-21m)

**Access:** Boat

**Expertise Rating:** Novice

Go down the slope to the staghorn coral flats. You'll find lots of chromis and an intact, upside-down Japanese Zero that was shot down during WWII. The plane rests at about 60ft and its guns and wings are still in place. A look underneath the cockpit reveals a large school of small glassy sweepers. Look for leaf fish in the engine compartment.

The propeller on the upside-down fighter is still intact.

## 24 | *Teshio Maru*

This Japanese freighter was sunk apparently trying to escape bombing by heading north to the main channel. The fore and aft damage was likely caused by the hits that sunk the ship, which now rests on its starboard side. As its port side is only 45ft from the surface, the wreck is subject to swells and gets shaken up during big storms. Despite this, there's good coral growth around the ship's bridge and on the port side. Intricate, broadly sprawling platter corals provide protective cover to small juvenile fish. Though the engine room was blasted open by salvagers, it is wise to stay out of it, as the whole area is unstable.

The *Teshio* is one of the fishiest wrecks in Palau, with schools of blackbar barracuda and striped skipjack joining

**Location:** 5 miles northeast of Palau Pacific Resort

**Depth Range:** 45-90ft (14-27m)

**Access:** Boat

**Expertise Rating:** Novice

various grouper species that live in the acropora corals. The mast has a lot of blue chromis busily flitting about and anemones are found at various intervals. A large, solitary barracuda also visits the ship. The water is much clearer here than at most of Palau's shipwrecks—on a good day you can see the entire wreck from the surface while snorkeling.

The engine room of the *Teshio* is filled with pipes and wreckage.

## 25 Jake Floatplane

This floatplane, an Aichi E13A or Jake-type reconnaissance seaplane, is one of the most intact plane wrecks in Micronesia. It sits mostly upright in shallow water not far north of the Meyuns seaplane ramp. Its wings and one float are still intact, and some of the window glass is still in place. The other, coral-encrusted float rests nearby. The wreck is surrounded by a coral garden and small sea whips and other encrusting marine life is found all over the plane.

A resident batfish that lives beneath the fuselage will often pose for photographers. Good macrophotography subjects include whitecap shrimp in razor corals and colorful juvenile tropicals in the coral heads.

**Location:** North of Meyuns seaplane ramp

**Depth Range:** 35-50ft (11-15m)

**Access:** Boat

**Expertise Rating:** Novice

Diver shines a light on the Jake's resident batfish.

# 26 | Chandelier Cave

Chandelier Cave is a real departure from reef diving. This shallow cave has a high ceiling that rises above the water level, allowing divers to surface, talk and even take off diving gear to walk around some of the many chambers.

**Location:** Rock Islands near Koror

**Depth Range:** 10-35ft (3-11m)

**Access:** Boat

**Expertise Rating:** Intermediate

Underwater, you enter the cave through a jungled undercut at about 20 to 25ft. Take special care to stay off of the ocean floor, which is silt-covered and stirs up easily. The light at the entrance is your exit reference, so it is especially important to keep the water clear.

Giant stalactites and clear water make this shallow dive spectacular.

It is pitch-black inside without a light. Stalactites and stalagmites can abruptly halt your progress, so don't enter without a dependable flashlight. Once inside, you'll find a limestone fantasyland with an upper layer of crystal-clear freshwater giving the impression of endless visibility. The clarity allows you to easily see the limestone formations.

You'll arrive at the first chamber after a short swim. Here, huge dripstones hang from the ceiling. You can get out of the water here and explore a small tunnel. In all, there are four air chambers connected by underwater tunnels that lead back to a large area where divers can again doff gear, get out of the water and walk around. The beauty of the dripstones and the chandelier-like forms make this a favorite novelty dive. The reef outside is also worth exploring, as there are some unusual fish, including mandarinfish, dragonets and colorful gobies.

## 27  *Ryuko Maru*

This interesting wreck lies just a stone's throw south of the Palau Pacific Resort, sandwiched between the south end of Ngargol Island and northwestern shore of Ngerekebesang Island. The ship is covered in black coral and full of skipjacks and lionfish. The wire and black corals adorning the wreck are full of tiny baitfish during plankton blooms. Also look for various pipefish that seem to reside happily in wreck habitats. Other sea

**Location:** South end Ngargol Island

**Depth Range:** 60-120ft (18-33m)

**Access:** Boat

**Expertise Rating:** Intermediate

life heavily encrusting the ship includes clams, jagged oysters and encrusting

Part of the *Ryuko*'s telegraph stand rests on the upper bridge.

sponges. Some brilliant golden gorgonians grow on the edges of the holds.

It is a pleasant over-swim and some parts can be easily penetrated. The bow sits at about 70ft with the deck dipping to 90ft, and it plummets to 120ft inside the holds. The holds are mostly empty—the cargo was either salvaged or the holds were empty when the ship was hit. A direct hit from an aerial bomb during the Desecrate 1 air raid of March 1944 caused some of the damage, especially around the bridge. A portion of what looks like the ship's compass stand is found on the bridge's first level, and the machine gun sits buried in the heavy silt. Bombs are found nearby in shallower water. The engine room is now open and accessible to divers, after it was blasted by salvagers so the boilers could be removed. The midships area burned heavily before the ship sank, so there is little wood left. Another nice feature of the ship is the outer passageway that runs along both sides of the lower bridge and accesses the various quarters and the engine room catwalk.

## 28  Amatsu Maru

The *Amatsu Maru* was one of the newer ships that came to rest on Palau's ocean floor, and has become one of its best wreck dives. It is heavily covered with corals, is a haven for fish and hasn't been heavily salvaged. The ship was built during WWII and sank close to Koror during the Desecrate 1 air raid. The 500-yard-long tanker is deeper than most Palau shipwrecks, with a deck depth averaging between 90 and 110ft. This, combined with sometimes-limited visibility, makes planning essential.

**Location:** Ngederrak Lagoon, south Ngargol Island

**Depth Range:** 70-130ft (21-40m)

**Access:** Boat

**Expertise Rating:** Intermediate

The *Amatsu* has a split superstructure, a pumphouse and catwalks that cover the piping. Look for unusual and dense invertebrate sea life on the catwalks.

This ship is in an area that is normally protected and free of currents, inviting marine life to settle down and stay for a while. Often called the Black Coral Wreck, the *Amatsu* is encrusted with trees

The derrick of this oiler is covered in marine life.

of golden, wispy, low-light black coral that grow so thickly in places that it is difficult to enter the passages. Adorned with magnificent fins, a particular resident lionfish species, *Pterois volitans*, feeds on the clear baitfish that seek shelter in the black coral branches.

A hawkfish rests in the black coral.

You can poke around and explore many places, such as the spacious but silty forecastle, which can be entered easily. A light is necessary to explore the interior areas.

## Natural Light Photography

People often go diving, see all of the brilliant colors of the fantastic undersea world, then eventually want to capture them on film. After all, if you can shoot a camera on land, why not underwater? Well, not quite...

Water works as a heavy-duty filter, cutting down exposure or light, filtering colors and generally making things move around a lot. The way to overcome some of this is to use artificial light, or a strobe flash.

For anyone not wanting to go to the expense of buying a flash, in the right location, some of Palau's reefs are colorful enough to get nice shots without artificial light. The Rock Islands' shallow upper reef walls and sandy flats are reflective enough to provide nice photos, snorkeling in 2 to 4ft.

No strobes were used in taking this picture.

Natural light is also good for taking pictures of large subjects and large animals. Strobes only reach about 6ft in the water before they are ineffective, so sharks, giant manta rays, whale sharks and shipwrecks cannot be covered well with any lighting system.

Use a reasonable shutter speed, around $\frac{1}{60}$ or $\frac{1}{125}$, to properly freeze your subject. Try to have the sun at your back or high overhead. If the subject is moving, pan with it. If it is a shipwreck, steady yourself, then squeeze the trigger.

# 29 *Chuyo Maru*

In 1990, wreck explorers Francis Toribiong and Klaus Lindemann took a morning boat trip to an old anchorage site near Koror to check out the sea floor with a depth finder. It was unlikely that they would find a wreck so close to a major population center, especially since the area was never really fished.

**Location:** Near Malakal anchorage

**Depth Range:** 30-120ft (9-36m)

**Access:** Boat

**Expertise Rating:** Intermediate

The two had been searching for and exploring local wrecks all week, and were at the end of their safe diving time. Then they saw what looked to be a large wreck on the finder screen so Toribiong jumped in to explore. At first he saw nothing, but then discovered the *Chuyo* when he started to ascend.

This coral- and fish-laden wreck is still in fine shape. The bridge is at 70ft and the deck is at 90ft. The bridge can be explored on several levels. It is very silty, so take photos when you arrive, before it gets too stirred up. Even if you move slowly and use caution to keep conditions favorable, your air bubbles alone can cause a rain of silt. Look for the ship's telegraph, which is intact but fallen over in the bridge's navigation area. A resident school of sharpnose barracuda especially likes the bridge aft areas.

The tops of the masts (the crosstrees) are gardens of corals and sponges, attracting various schools of fusiliers and other fish. Cock's comb oysters are thick on this wreck. The current off the bow makes it popular with schooling fish. The taut anchor chain stretches down to the sand. Farther back, forward of the bridge on the port side, a large anchor sits on the deck.

The coral-covered compass of the Chuyo still stands on the bridge.

# 30 Helmet Wreck

This ship is just minutes away from most Koror dive shops and offers so much it may take a couple of dives to fully explore. It has been given a number of monikers, including Mystery Wreck and Depth Charge Wreck. Experts are still trying to identify the ship, as it was used by the Japanese during the war, but does not appear to be Japanese-built. It is a fairly recent discovery by wreck expert Dan Bailey, and is a treasure trove of war materials and ship artifacts.

Helmet Wreck—named for its cargo of helmets that are now fused together

**Location:** Malakal Harbor

**Depth Range:** 28-95ft (7.5-29m)

**Access:** Boat

**Expertise Rating:** Novice

after being in the ocean for so long—sits on a sloping bank with the stern at 50ft and the bow at about 100ft. It appears to be a new ship, as an inspection of its engine room shows a triple expansion,

Fused helmets in the aft hold give the wreck its name.

single shaft steam engine—a lot of power for a such a small ship. Oddly, the ship's coal bin (used to fuel the engines and cook stove) holds little coal, indicating that it may not have been in use at the time it went down.

The ship has three holds, one in the stern and two in the bow, with the ship's superstructure and engine room in between. The rear hold displays massive damage from an obviously powerful explosion. The starboard deck and side plating was blown back, curling until it almost touches the intact sides and deck of the bow. The bow gun was jarred from its mount by the explosion and lies on its side. The companion ladder and platform ladder are doubled over and the mast ladder has fallen onto the gun platform. The mast crosstree is missing. The top of the bow mast extends to within 28ft of the surface and is overgrown with corals and encrusting marine life.

The forward section of the aft hold is packed with round canisters about the size of thirty-gallon drums. These are depth charges, thus the name Depth Charge Wreck. This hold also contains encrusted carbine rifles, ammunition, stacks of helmets and gas masks. The bridge floorboards have disappeared, but the helm and the brass ring of the wheel (marine worms eat the wood, leaving only the brass) are present and laying on their sides. The galley has pots, pans, bottles, cups, dishes, claret glasses, a coal burning stove and other utensils. Equipment is still in place in a small radio room. The closed skylights protect the engine room from heavy silting. The engine and winch remain in fine shape and the brass gauges in the boiler area are still readable. The ship's stack (one of the first things to rust and tumble off sunken ships) sits on the reef along the starboard side.

The forward holds contain assorted electrical parts and fixtures. It is possible to swim from the center hold to the forward hold, as the partition between decks is gone. The most notable pieces of cargo are three large airplane engines in the forward hold. The boson's locker in the bow contains some beautiful storm lanterns and a taffrail log that any seasoned navigator would love to have a look at.

## 31 Brown Corner

This area near the M-Dock in Medalaii was jokingly dubbed Brown Corner in reference to its extreme contrast to the famous Blue Corner. It became a popular muck-diver's site when marine photographers David Doubilet and James D. Watt discovered it to be a haven for mandarin-fish. These rare critters come out at dusk, so bring a light if you want to see them.

The easiest entry is via the steps at the M-Dock (near the hotel entrance). The steps can be slippery, so be careful. The entire dive can be done in less

**Location:** Marina Hotel, M-Dock

**Depth Range:** 0-40ft (0-12m)

**Access:** Shore

**Expertise Rating:** Novice

than 6ft by just poking along the old Japanese wall.

This site holds many macro surprises in addition to the mandarins. Other tiny creatures include the banded fantail pipefish, cardinalfish, frogfish and spotted gobies. A variety of small crabs and shrimp live in the rocks. The nearby silty slope has a variety of tridacna clams, cuttlefish and a resident sea snake. The outer reef near the channel is home to parrotfish, a school of jacks and batfish, and many crocodile needlefish.

This is best dived at high tide. At low tide, the boat wake causes the silt to stir up, reducing visibility and causing backscatter in pho-

tos. At incoming tide, as many as a dozen eagle rays will come around the corner and into the marina.

A fantail pipefish in the Brown Corner shallows.

## Mysterious Mating Mandarinfish

The tiny mandarinfish has been a favorite of photographers and biologists for decades because of its brilliant green-orange pattern. But the reclusive habits and odd habitat make these fish very hard to find. Mandarinfish like still water and normally hide in the deep

recesses of the reef or in coral rubble. They become romantic and active around dusk, when you can see them swimming to the surface, mating in oblivious pairs. The male's the one with a beautiful elongated dorsal fin.

Sometimes, on cloudy days, the mandarinfish can be faked out, thinking it is dusk. Also remember, if you see one, there is probably a whole family in the area. They are territorial, so if you find them, you can usually return to the same spot to photograph them evening after evening.

## 32 Kesebekuu Channel (Lighthouse)

Kesebekuu Channel is home to a WWII shipwreck of a Japanese refrigeration ship, and lots of fish and rich coral growth, especially in the shallow upper reef areas. Expect a current to be running through here most of the time, ranging from slight at slack tide to quite brisk at tide change. The dive is normally started near Channel Marker 6 as divers first descend to the small wreck.

**Location:** East of Malakal Harbor

**Depth Range:** 20-80ft (6-24m)

**Access:** Boat

**Expertise Rating:** Intermediate

The ship near one of the channel markers in Kesebekuu Channel is often referred to as the **Channel Marker Wreck**. The ship's large holds have coils that would've been used to refrigerate fish, indicating that this ship was a Japanese fishing boat before being reconfigured into a sub chaser during the war. The wreck sits with a slight list at about 80ft at the bottom of a current-filled sandy channel. The ship is large enough for a diver to duck behind and be perfectly sheltered from the current. As you descend along the slope you'll see incredible stands of green tube corals. At night, the extended coral polyps make magnificent photo subjects.

The deck is covered with ever-increasing growths of soft corals and sea fans, and immense angelfish hover around the wreck. Flurries of brightly colored tropical fish feed madly in the current that passes over the top of the ship.

The upper cabin area is small but easily explored. The gun from the small gun platform on the bow has been removed,

as has the propeller. The rudder has disintegrated, but three supports still stick out the back of the ship.

If you don't feel like fighting the current to see the ship (the current varies from weak to ripping, so check the tide changes), the shallow reef as you move up the channel wall is an incredible dive in itself. Cuttlefish huddle over carpets of staghorn coral. Silver and blue chromis join golden anthias in these immense spreads of coral and feed with wild and colorful abandon. Numerous table and platter corals surround some large sea anemones hosting the accompanying clownfish. Green, white and brown tunicate colonies spread out across this filter-feeders' haven.

This spot is also considered a great night dive, with colorful crinoids and accompanying clingfish and squat lobster, basket stars, many varieties of nudibranchs and flatworms coming out at night to feed.

The colorful nudibranch *notodoris minor* can be seen in this channel.

Green tube corals and soft corals flourish in the channel's currents.

# 33 Iro Maru

The *Iro* is perhaps the best-known and one of the most popular shipwrecks in Palau. It is just a short distance from Koror and is normally protected from winds and rough seas. It is a shallow dive to the deck, and is beautifully overgrown with many forms of sessile marine life.

**Location:** Urukthapel Bay

**Depth Range:** 50-120ft (15-36m)

**Access:** Boat

**Expertise Rating:** Novice

The *Iro* was an oiler, and you can still see a small oil slick in the area, as some kind of petroleum product still leaks after all these years. It doesn't seem to hinder the marine growth on the ship, however. The first thing divers note upon descent is the schooling yellowtails around the masts. The crosstrees are heavily encrusted with hard corals and oysters. On rare occasions, shellfish spawn and fusiliers gather around for a free meal.

Divers are likely to be greeted by a resident school of batfish, which make marvelous photographic subjects. They faithfully follow divers like a pack of puppies, dining on the small shrimp and other critters that get kicked up by the divers' fins.

Built in 1922, the *Iro* was a victim of a submarine torpedo attack prior to the Desecrate 1 air raid. The bow displays a large crescent where a torpedo hit, but this is not the damage that caused her to sink. She was actually downed by an aerial bomb farther aft, but the well-defined torpedo hole is the spot you can swim though. It is now heavily overgrown with black coral and sponges. The thick

Spawning razor clams along the bridge of the *Iro*.

anchor chain found nearby is home to a variety of marine invertebrates.

The bow gun is mounted on a huge platform, which is also overgrown with delicate, wispy black coral trees and fish and invertebrate life. The aft ship has a number of overgrown pipes, derricks and a beautiful mast configuration. The galley is also back here but is pretty thick in silt and should be explored only by prepared and experienced wreck divers.

Like many wrecks in Palau, the *Iro* was salvaged after the war, but there is still lots to see. More than one dive is recommended for a really close inspection.

## 34 Gozan Maru

The *Gozan Maru* was discovered in 1984. The nearly intact wreck has not been positively identified, but is believed to be the *Gozan*.

The ship went down on its side and now lists heavily to port. The shallowest part of the hull resembles a reef. Many types of coral have latched on to this wreck, from brain, platter and star corals, to large leather corals. Purple-tipped anemones with skunk clownfish are scattered

**Location:** West Urukthapel Island

**Depth Range:** 25-80ft (6-24m)

**Access:** Boat

**Expertise Rating:** Novice

throughout. Small schools of barracuda roam the wreck and at times approach

A lionfish moves along the deck of the *Gozan*.

divers, getting close enough to be photographed.

The foremast is a haven for marine invertebrates. Tridacna clams nestle between corals and one-stripe clownfish hover near large colonies of bubble anemones. Clams, oysters, whip corals and bulb corals congregate on the shallow mast. Dense schools of fish, especially small basslets, add a splash of color. Swimming through the ship can be a little disorienting, as it lists heavily to port.

The holds are empty, but the second hold shows the damage that sunk the ship. The explosion apparently tore the bottom plates loose and the result is a jagged, inwardly bent, gaping hole large enough for a diver to swim through. The upper bridge and rear are worth investigating, but stay out of the engine room, as it is extremely dark and rife with pipes and loose wires. Though the ship's interior is generally free of any noticeable current, the presence of filter-feeders—sea fans and other gorgonians, soft corals and stinging hydroids—indicates that some water flows through here.

Nearby is the completely blown-apart *Kamikaze Maru.* The shock wave from this ship's massive explosion may explain some of the *Gozan*'s damage. Some explosives are still in the remains of the *Kamikaze*'s forward holds, so that ship is best left alone.

## Ulong Island Dive Sites

Ulong Island is an excellent place to visit between dives at Siaes or Ulong Channel because of its expansive beach and historical nature. Hike high up the cliffs and

Ulong Island as seen from Koror.

you'll find caves with petroglyphs left by ancient Palauans. The hike up is not for the faint-hearted—and don't look down until you get to the cave.

In the jungle at the southwest end of the beach sits a monument to the *Antelope*, the ill-fated ship that wrecked on the reef, bringing Captain Henry Wilson of the East India Company and the first Europeans to Palau.

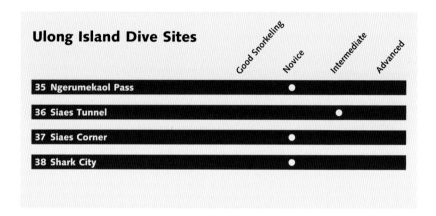

| Ulong Island Dive Sites | Good Snorkeling | Novice | Intermediate | Advanced |
|---|---|---|---|---|
| 35 Ngerumekaol Pass | | ● | | |
| 36 Siaes Tunnel | | | ● | |
| 37 Siaes Corner | | ● | | |
| 38 Shark City | | ● | | |

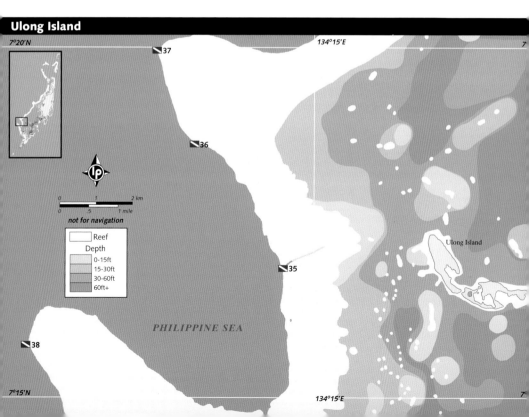

Ulong Island

# 35 Ngerumekaol Pass

If you had to be shipwrecked, Ulong Island is the kind of tropical paradise you would hope to be stranded on. Birds soar above the beautiful sandy beaches and looming cliffs. Tall coconut trees and rich, green vegetation decorate the landscape. Ulong was, in fact, where Captain Henry Wilson wrecked the *Antelope*, thereby "discovering" Palau for the western world. A plaque on the island's beach tells this tale.

**Location:** West of Ulong Island

**Depth Range:** 20-80ft (6-24m)

**Access:** Boat

**Expertise Rating:** Novice

West of Ulong is Ngerumekaol Pass, one of the best drift dives in Palau. Huge coral heads dot the steep slopes on each side, and the soft- and fan-coral cover looks like it was placed by an expert landscape architect. Both brilliantly colored and jet-black crinoids filter-feed during the daytime. Big and occasionally exotic fish, like the spectacular threadfin pompano, which usually inhabit the open ocean, frequent this spillway. It is a popular resting place for hawksbill turtles and a spawning ground for large groupers. Protected by law, the groupers have actually been seen schooling here, which is rare for these normally solitary fish.

During the tide change the fish action is excellent. Whitetip and grey

The Pass is known for its large lettuce corals.

reef sharks are common, especially at the mouth of the channel. Even a tiger shark has been reported. More than one diver has had a pesky remora leave a shark or turtle and try to attach itself during a channel dive.

A remora rests on a whitetip shark.

One of the largest stands of lettuce corals you'll ever see is in the middle of this pass. Anemones nestle inside and, at night, beautiful basket stars come out to the edge of the coral lips to catch particles in the current.

Ngerumekaol averages about 50 to 60ft depths but can get as deep as 80ft in some spots. It is an ideal second dive and an exciting night dive.

## 36 Siaes Tunnel

The Siaes Tunnel, west of the Ulong Channel along the outer barrier reef, is one of the most exciting dives Palau has to offer. The mammoth underground cave, known for its sheer wall and active marine life, is home to a multitude of sea inhabitants, from wispy black coral trees to sleeping sharks.

Boats normally anchor in about 15ft of water at the edge of the Siaes Corner, which is a also a great experience. The tunnel entrance is not visible from the surface. Divers drift down through a resident population of pyramid butterflyfish, and descend along the wall. The electric-crimson and sun-gold gorgonian fans quiver in the current that runs gently along the wall. Schools of weighty bumphead parrotfish course the area, moving vertically along the cliff face.

When you reach 60ft, you'll see the tunnel entrance. A sandy bottom comes clearly into view at this point, unlike

**Location:** West of Ulong Island

**Depth Range:** 80-130ft (24-40m)

**Access:** Boat

**Expertise Rating:** Intermediate

most of the wall, which drops to incredible depths. At about 90ft, the mouth of the tunnel is inviting, but with depths averaging 100 to 130ft, this cave dive teeters on the edge of safe sport diving limits.

It is not unusual to see a large ray rising from the sandy bottom of the entrance. Inside, a school of crevalle jacks is likely to swoop past your light to satisfy their curiosity. A giant grouper has also been reported here. The roof of the cave is forested in black coral, while the floor is covered in gorgonians. Reef and whitetip sharks use

Divers approach the entrance to Siaes Tunnel.

the cave to rest. They like to sleep in a side opening of the tunnel. This room, found to the right as you exit, is at 100ft and has a window exit to the sea. You can see it by natural light, but a dive light is helpful. Moray eels and usually a sleeping leopard nurse shark are near the darker reaches. Exit through a wreath of large sea fans growing from the top and sides of the window, and ascend up the wall for your safety decompression stop.

A crinoid adorns a rare white form of black coral.

## 37 Siaes Corner

A visit to this corner can start with a dive at Siaes Tunnel, and then a drift to this site or you can just dive the corner and save yourself the excess swimming. This site is not often visited, but it is an excellent drift dive when the tide is moving. At tide change, pelagic life can be very good, including eagle rays, grey reef sharks and barracudas.

**Location:** West of Ulong Island

**Depth Range:** 35-130ft (11-40m)

**Access:** Boat

**Expertise Rating:** Novice

During your drift at the corner, you'll see lots of fish life along the steep drop-off. Cleaning stations attract beautiful surgeonfish, which turn powder-blue when they are being cleaned. Look for clouds of small tropicals, including the active pyramid butterflyfish, bigeyes, bluestripe fusiliers and squirrelfish. A variety of basket stars, colorful sea fans and sea whips with commensal shrimp spring out from the wall to feed in the current.

## 38 Shark City

This wall and drift dive is one of the best big-fish dives in Palau. It was named Shark City many years ago by the U.S. *Skin Diver* magazine. Until the "discovery" of Blue Corner in the late 1980s, this was Palau's premier dive. Now, it is not visited very often, which is a shame, as it is a really fine site. Like most hot spots in Palau, the most big-critter action occurs when the tide is moving, so time your dive accordingly.

This point of the barrier reef actually has four fingers, which harbor a variety of marine life. One has a resident school of barracuda, another hosts schooling jacks. Grey reef sharks are known to loi-

**Location:** Southwest barrier reef

**Depth Range:** 20-120ft (6-36m)

**Access:** Boat

**Expertise Rating:** Novice

ter here, along with large sea turtles. The sea fans, soft corals and other invertebrate growth here is quite good, and some large, colorful sea anemones dot the upper wall and reef. An occasional hammerhead, sailfish or marlin will stray in, so keep an eye on the blue water.

Schooling blackbar barracuda are frequently seen at Shark City.

# Babeldaob & Northern Reefs Dive Sites

Despite healthy reefs and lots of big fish, Palau's remote northern reaches are not dived much. The steep drop-offs and the exposed passages in the south draw divers away from this area, keeping the reefs relatively free from divers. But this is a great area to see schools of large pelagic fish. Babeldaob's ecosystem, fed by the nutrients of the Babeldaob rivers, is one of the most varied in the world. You can also explore some seldom visited shipwrecks here.

KEVIN DAVIDSON

Kayangel Atoll

Possibly the world's most scenic atoll—Kayangel Atoll—sits about 10 miles (16km) from Babeldaob's northern tip. Excursions to Kayangel atoll are best accessed by live-aboards especially chartered to explore the north, or by camping overnight on a nearby island. Kayangel's channels are unprotected; winds and surge can make the trip a rough ride, but the scenery, marine life and pristine reefs make the trip well worthwhile.

| Babeldaob & Northern Reefs Dive Sites | Good Snorkeling | Novice | Intermediate | Advanced |
|---|:---:|:---:|:---:|:---:|
| 39 The Seaplanes | ● | ● | | |
| 40 Blue Sea Lake | ● | ● | | |
| 41 *Kibi Maru* | | | ● | |
| 42 *Wakatake* Destroyer | ● | | | ● |
| 43 Devil's Playground | | | ● | |
| 44 Wild West Coral Gardens | | ● | | |
| 45 Ngeremlengui Channel | | | ● | |
| 46 Devilfish City | | | ● | |
| 47 Kayangel Atoll | ● | | ● | |
| 48 Velasco Reef | | | | ● |

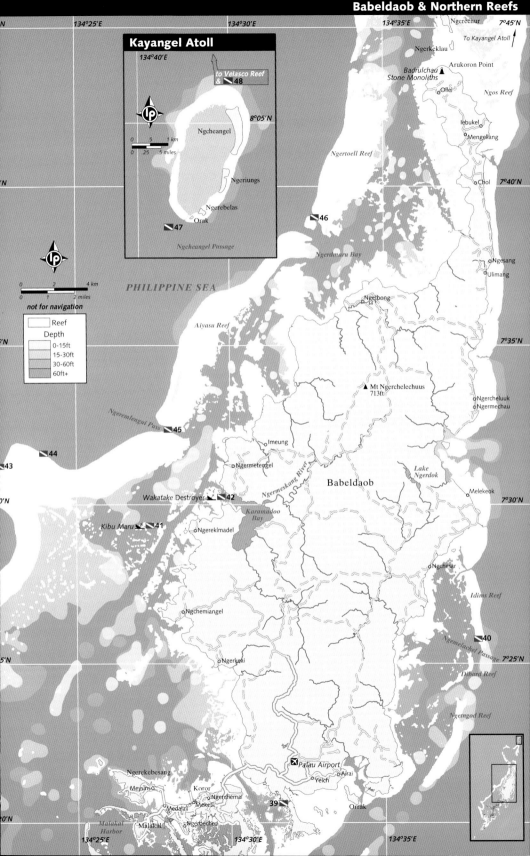

## Kayangel Atoll

134°40'E

to Velasco Reef & ◹ 48

8°05'N

Ngcheangel

Ngeriungs

Ngerebelas

Orak

◹ 47

0   .5   1 km
0   .25   .5 miles

*Ngcheangel Passage*

**PHILIPPINE SEA**

*Aiyasu Reef*

0   2   4 km
0   1   2 miles

*not for navigation*

| Reef |
|------|
| Depth |

0-15ft
15-30ft
30-60ft
60ft+

*Ngeremlengui Pass* ◹ 45

◹ 44

43

*Wakatake Destroyer* ◹ 42

*Kibu Maru* ◹ 41

Ngereklmadel

Imeung

Ngermetengel

*Ngermeskang River*

*Karamadoo Bay*

Ngchemiangel

Ngerkeai

**Babeldaob**

▲ Mt Ngerchelechuus
713ft

*Lake Ngerdok*

Ngchesar

134°25'E   7°45'N

Ngerechur

To Kayangel Atoll ↑

Ngerkeklau

Arukoron Point

*Badrulchau Stone Monoliths* ▲

Ollei

*Ngos Reef*

Iebukel

Mengellang

Chol   7°40'N

*Ngertoell Reef*

Ngesang

Ulimang

◹ 46

*Ngerdmaru Bay*

Ngeibong

7°35'E

Ngercheluuk
Ngermechau

Melekeok   7°30'N

*Idims Reef*

◹ 40

*Ngemelachel Passage*   7°25'N

*Dibard Reef*

*Ngeingod Reef*

Ngerekebesang

Meyuns

Koror

Ngerchemal

Medalaii   Mekeii

Malakal

Ngerbeched

*Malakal Harbor*

✈ Palau Airport

Yeich   Airai

Orrak

◹ 39

134°25'E   134°30'E   134°35'E

# 39 The Seaplanes

The remnants of at least two Jake-Aichi floatplanes lie just beneath the water on the Babeldaob side of the KB Bridge. Aichi began building Jake floatplanes in 1938, so these planes were virtually brand new when WWII started. Jake airplanes had two principle roles: to attack or spy. Attack planes carried three crewmembers and a cargo of bombs, but were rather slow. The Jake also served as a long-range reconnaissance plane, which suited it much better. They could also berth easily in the lagoons.

**Location:** Southern Babeldaob

**Depth Range:** 0-20ft (0-6m)

**Access:** Boat

**Expertise Rating:** Novice

One plane is scattered, nestled in some rocky islands, but the prop and engine are visible. The better Jake wreck settled across from a cave. The wings stretch out broadly, though they have little coral growth. The engine has fallen forward, probably from its own weight, but the pilot's seat is still intact. The plane's floats are also visible, with one still in place under a wing. The metal can be jagged, so take care when exploring these sites. It is best to come here at high tide.

The shallow seaplanes can be seen on snorkel.

# 40   Blue Sea Lake

Blue Sea Lake is an inner reef site just off Ngeschar village on the tip of the barrier reef. The "lake" (actually a blue hole) is surrounded by a shallow coral reef, but opens to a wide and deep hole with a sandy, somewhat silty bottom full of nutrients carried by the currents from the nearby mangroves.

This is a good place to see lobster. Also, look for foraging sand and eagle rays. The hole's relative protection means a safe home to lots of juvenile sea life, including young barracuda and skipjacks. Many small tropicals seek shelter in the corals and along the lake walls, and shoals of red snappers can also appear. A wall area is patrolled by whitetip reef sharks.

The channel and cut near Blue Sea Lake is also interesting. Dolphins and pilot whales come into the mouth to feed on schools of fish. Sightings of the rare Palauan dugong have also been reported outside the barrier reef. Again, this is a

**Location:** Eastern Barrier Reef

**Depth Range:** 5-85ft (1.5-26m)

**Access:** Boat

**Expertise Rating:** Novice

part of Palau divers rarely visit, so enjoy the opportunity to see some of the stunning northeast coast of the archipelago's largest island.

A conger eel pokes its head out at night.

## Sunken Village & Milad's Magical Tree

A site referred to as Sunken Village, on the east side of Babeldaob, north of Melekeok and south of Ngiwal, is the legendary site of the submerged of Ngibtal Village. You'll often see this popular Palauan legend depicted in prints and storyboards.

According to the story, Milad, the granddaughter of Matmikiak, lived on the islet of Ngibtal off the Babeldaob mainland. Milad possessed a magic breadfruit tree with a hol

low trunk that reached down into the lagoon. Occasionally, waves forced fish up through the trunk, providing enough to feed the entire village.

In time, the village people became jealous of Milad's good fortune (even though she was feeding them), and one day took clamshell axes and cut down the girl's magic tree. The ocean poured through the stump and flooded the island, sinking the village. No remnants verify the existence of this mythical sunken village, where, oddly, only a lone tree stump remains.

# 41 *Kibi Maru*

This large freighter can be an excellent dive for those wanting to see many forms of encrusting marine life. For the ship-wreck buff, this is a unique log entry, as the ship sits upside-down but can still be explored.

**Location:** Inner channel west/central Babeldaob

**Depth Range:** 20-90ft (6-27m)

**Access:** Boat

**Expertise Rating:** Intermediate

The *Kibi* was strafed in WWII action that led to its demise. The ship ran aground on a reef near the West Passage exit, where it was salvaged after the war. It later slid down into deeper water, coming to rest upside-down at 90ft. The main hindrance here is the current. Try to time this dive when the tide is high and slack to get the least current and best visibility.

The upper reef has lots of acropora corals and small tropicals. A dive down the steep slope reveals large branching evergreen tubastrea coral.

Wreck divers and invertebrate seekers will certainly like this ship. One entire side is covered in a mass of encrusting corals, sponges, fans, sea whips and other invertebrates that are good for macrophotography (albeit challenging because of the currents). Black coral grows both on the seafloor and inside of the ship. Golden sea fans and some large soft corals bloom on the *Kibi*'s stern.

The bow, which is bent and somewhat buckled, holds a veritable forest of sea whips. Critters, such as pipefish, razor clams and sea stars reside among the whip branches.

You can enter the ship's inner sanctum through the starboard side (away from the western channel wall). Divers are advised not to enter the bridge areas, poop or anything on top of the deck (now crushed and upside-down), as they are unstable.

The deep and dark inner hold of the *Kibi Maru*.

## 42  *Wakatake* Destroyer

The ship historians believe to be the *Wa-katake* Destroyer lies in a channel in west-central Babeldaob. It's not a dive for everyone, as there can be tricky currents, low visibility and a lot of wreckage, but adventurous divers will find it worth exploring. Try to dive it at slack high tide, when the visibility can reach up to 25ft.

**Location:** Karamadoo Bay, west Babeldaob

**Depth Range:** 0-70ft (0-21m)

**Access:** Boat

**Expertise Rating:** Advanced

The wreck starts on the shoreline at Karamadoo Bay, where shore-hugging clams and mussels poke above the surface at low tide. Parts of the ship appear in just 2ft, reaching down to the bottom, which flattens out at around 70ft before dropping deeper.

This wreck is broken up but still intact enough to probe. Take care not to stir up the heavy silt while exploring the openings, which are havens for sweetlips, snappers and large groupers. The ship still has its stern gun, which points downward, as the ship's stern is on its side. The 14cm shells sit on the seafloor in what is left of their seaworm-eaten wooden boxes.

Francis Toribiong examines a sextant from this site.

## 43  Devil's Playground

This site is just south of West Passage on a point of the barrier reef. Currents can be tricky here but, especially during the flat summer months, this corner and reef area beckons diver exploration. Dugongs swim into this pass and large mantas feed with the changing tides. Devil's Playground is well known for its eagle rays, and sleeping nurse sharks are commonly found hiding under the large coral heads. This is also a favorite place to find lobster.

**Location:** West-central outer reef, west Babeldaob

**Depth Range:** 30-130ft (9-40m)

**Access:** Boat

**Expertise Rating:** Intermediate

Large fish roam and sea whips dot the floor where the reef slopes down to a

Large schools of batfish course the upper reef.

current-swept plain, which leads to some deepwater drop-offs.

In the deeper, under-explored reaches, be ready for a visit from a grey shark or a fast-moving ray. Large, grazing Napoleon wrasse and schools of bumphead parrotfish can also be found here. Sprawling, migrating groups of spadefish and tangs are often found just off the lip of the wild, deep drop-offs that fall off into oblivion.

## 44  Wild West Coral Gardens

This broad pass on the western slopes of Ngeremlengui's outer reef is fed by a twin river system that flows into Karama-doo Bay. The bay then empties through a snaking channel into the southern Philippine Sea. The outer reefs just south of this pass are rarely dived and offer surprises at every turn.

The incredible nutrients flushed into the sea feed spectacular coral growth on the upper reef slopes. Deeper, yawning slopes, current-swept flats and deep undersea points and drop-offs provide a varied terrain that attracts some awesome marine life.

Diving here requires a calm day, and a high tide doesn't hurt. You need the calm because some of the best spots are outside the pass, and a little south along a reef point that juts into the open sea. Swells and storms can roll in quickly here, so if the weather looks threatening, save this dive for another day.

On those special days when the sea is calm and the sky is blue and windless,

**Location:** Outer reef, west-central Babeldaob

**Depth Range:** 20-80ft (6-24m)

**Access:** Boat

**Expertise Rating:** Novice

hop in. You won't get the sharp drop-offs of the south or the extremely clear water, but you can expect rich coral gardens and exciting visits by spotted, and rarer ornate eagle rays. An adult ornate eagle ray has an extremely long tail that makes it look like a living kite as it sails through the water.

In the shallower areas, look for the territorial clownfish in the various brightly colored hues of sea anemones. They sit on top of large coral heads, surrounded by clouds of fairy salmon, hot-pink basslets and electric blue chromis.

Healthy corals on this rarely dived site are home to colorful anthias and basslets.

## 45 Ngeremlengui Channel

This pass is located almost halfway up the west coast of Babeldaob. Two large rivers empty into the ocean near the pass, also known as West Passage. The rivers' rich nutrients feed the expansive mangrove forest, which is a hatchery for a wide variety of juvenile marine life. The nutrients also feed corals and large sea fans, tall stands of evergreen cup corals and soft corals that grow in a variety of brilliant hues. The mangroves are also the main home of Palau's saltwater crocodiles.

The current often runs swiftly, making it a drift dive. Hire an experienced boat driver who knows the reefs and can follow your bubbles and pick you up at the end of your dive.

The wall along the pass ranges from a sharp slope to totally vertical. There are even places in the wall that are undercut, providing overhangs with sea fans and

**Location:** West reef, central Babeldaob

**Depth Range:** 20-110ft (6-33m)

**Access:** Boat

**Expertise Rating:** Intermediate

black coral trees. These walls are current swept, resulting in hardier, but not necessarily lush, marine growth. Filter-feeders do well here, so look out for sea whips, crinoids and anemones.

Some sites along the wall, especially between the two red channel-markers, have sandy slopes. Many kinds of fusiliers like these walls—brilliant yellowtails and electric blues course by the outcroppings, providing a show of motion and color. Also look for huge schools of striped snapper. Sharks, Napoleon wrasse and dogtooth tuna swim in from the blue or hover near the channel floor.

The grey reef sharks can be very territorial here and not as laid back as those along the Blue Corner. If they start acting territorial, get out of their way by slowly ascending to a shallower depth.

This is the only place that a *mesekiu*, or Palauan dugong, has been photographed underwater. These sea cows are similar to Florida manatees but have adapted to resting in the open ocean during the day to avoid predation by hunters. At night they come into the shallows to munch on sea grasses. If you're lucky, a school of spinner dolphins may appear and give a show, leaping from the sea with acrobatic moves. It is a beautiful sight as the animals frolic, framed by the background of Babeldaob's majestic hillside jungles.

Heavy flow of nutrients nourish giant sea fans.

## Sirens of the Sea

Palau's dugong (*mesekiu* in Palauan) is one of the world's four surviving species of sirenians, or sea cows. Usually only seen in the bays and open ocean waters surrounding the archipelago, the dugongs munch primarily on sea grasses. In the northern Babeldaob waters, they live in the open ocean and come into the broad reef flats to reproduce and eat.

Today, the Palau dugong is a prime candidate for extinction, as it is a slow breeder and faces a variety of threats, including shark attacks, hunting and loss of habitat due to pollution. Recent studies in Palau show that the small population there seems to be holding its own, but any more predation will threaten the existence of the prized *mesekiu*.

## 46 Devilfish City

You can dive channels and visit a manta ray cleaning station at this site along the western coast of northern Babeldaob. The channel sides (at around 80ft) are lined with massive fields of sea whips, soft corals, sea fans and large stands of evergreen tubastrea corals. As with most channels that lead from mangrove to the sea, visibility here shifts with the tide. High slack tide has the least current, greatest visibility and is your best chance to see a congregation of mantas, as the rays don't like to work too hard when they are being cleaned.

Once the current increases, look for feeding and sometimes mating activity. Many other fish will become more active as the current strengthens, including rainbow runners, reef sharks, bumphead parrotfish and fusiliers.

There is one large coral head in the channel and another set of

**Location:** Ngerdmaru Channel, northwest Babeldaob

**Depth Range:** 30-80ft (9-24m)

**Access:** Boat

**Expertise Rating:** Intermediate

sea-fan-adorned coral heads in a flat area in shallower water. The mantas come in

A red sea fan marks the site of a cleaning station.

to clean at the far coral head (in about 45ft), which is easy to find—look for

Remoras swim with a manta.

hundreds of copper sweeper baitfish swirling around the coral head's gorgonians and soft corals. Butterflyfish and wrasse wait for the mantas. On a good day, the mantas line up like jets at an airport. They wait their turn and then hover while they get cleaned. Mantas don't like to be touched or chased, so find an unobtrusive place near the cleaning site and be as motionless as possible. The mantas come quite close and the cleaning continues for some time.

A drift out of the channel also brings nice surprises, such as schools of striped skipjack or shocking pink anemones sitting beside electric-blue tridacna clams.

## 47 Kayangel Atoll

One of the most beautiful and most photographed atolls in the world, Kayangel is the quintessential Pacific atoll, with a school of spinner dolphins living at the entrance to its variegated emerald,

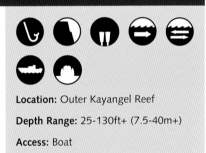

**Location:** Outer Kayangel Reef

**Depth Range:** 25-130ft+ (7.5-40m+)

**Access:** Boat

**Expertise Rating:** Intermediate

The tranquil inner lagoon at Kayangel.

turquoise and azure inner lagoon. The larger main and three smaller islands have idyllic beaches, lush palm and jungle growth, and sandy coasts with small stands of coral. Fewer than 100 people live on the main island and the other islands are uninhabited. Frigates, noddies, boobies, Pacific whitebirds and terns live along the beaches, or come to the islands to roost at night. The starry skies and lapping waves create an ideal atmosphere for an evening of relaxation before embarking on the next day's adventure.

The reef diving around Kayangel can be quite good, with pelagic action, large schools of fish and beautiful formations of corals. At **Virgin Sacrifice**, just south of Kayangel in the passage between the reef and the atoll, simply drift with the current for a long and pleasant dive. Whip corals and some gorgonian sea fans accent the current-swept drop-off, and table and platter corals dot the reeftop. Schools of brilliant yellow-stripe sweetlips, black snapper and yellowspot emperors swirl with schooling fish around the large coral heads. Also look for nudi-branchs and other invertebrate life. Be careful to watch what the current is doing, as it can easily take you away from the wall and out to open sea, effectively aborting your dive plan.

On the eastern outer reef, Kay-angel also has a **Blue Hole** that starts at around 80ft and runs down to 160ft through a chasm in the wall. The **Kayangel Wall**, also on the outer reef, can bring many thrills, including drift diving and the promise of pelagic life. Watch for silvertip sharks, grey reef sharks and other big fish. The area is known as a haven for golden cowries. The outer reef is not diveable much of the year, so if you get to the outer barrier reef on a calm day, cherish the moment and enjoy the dive.

The outer reefs hold schooling sweetlips and hard corals.

## 48 Velasco Reef

The extensive Velasco Reef in the open ocean just 20 miles north of Kayangel Atoll, almost to Ngulu, is a treasure trove of marine life. The reef rises to 60ft along its current-swept reaches and falls sharply into the blue.

Silvertip sharks congregate along the drop-offs, especially where coral life is thickest. These beautiful sharks, with silvery bodies and distinct white splotches on the tips of their dorsal and pectoral fins, vary in size from 2 to 10ft, getting bigger as you go deeper.

Silvertips' swimming action and un-abashed curiosity can be a bit unnerving.

**Location:** 20 miles North of Kayangel Atoll

**Depth Range:** 60-130ft (18-40m)

**Access:** Boat

**Expertise Rating:** Advanced

They approach divers quickly and sometimes closely. As long as they approach one at a time, they seem to be no problem, but you might reevaluate the situation when the sharks form a wolf-like pack.

To find these sharks, look for their food sources (birds and schools of fish) at the surface. One site where they are particularly abundant is **Silvertip City**, toward the north end of Velasco Reef. A dive here is always a current ride. Roll along the eastern slope where sapphire triggerfish (called blue tangs) dot the reef pass. Lone formations of vase and porites coral, delicate sea whips and fans can be found. Watch for silvertips coming in from the blue. There is also a good chance of seeing other sharks here, like grey reef sharks, bronze whalers, oceanic whitetip sharks and even tiger sharks. Blue marlin and sailfish are seen occasionally, and rainbow runners also like this terrain. Keep a lookout for bumphead parrotfish, schooling hammerheads and congregations of nurse sharks.

**Shark Central,** along the central eastern reef just south of Silvertip City, is another site that is loaded with coral and fish. The sloping drop-off starts at 90ft before falling into the deep blue. Excellent visibility allows you to see the cave and coral-covered ledges deep down at 200ft. Larger pelagic sharks and ocean-going fish, including schools of tuna, will likely pay a visit.

Massive bumphead parrotfish roam the reeftops like buffalo on the Great Plains. Large schools of rainbow runners, sweetlips, bluestripe and yellotail fusiliers, yellowspot emperors, black snappers and lots of other fish inhabit these reefs. The chance of seeing pelagics, such as wahoo and king mackerel, is also good.

Look for large, healthy stands of cabbage and vase corals, and look for small invertebrates living in the blades of deepwater sea grasses. At the south end of Velasco is **Ngeruangel Reef**, whose sand spit breaks the surface. Five shipwrecks were found here, but they've either broken up or been salvaged. Remnants of the *Samidare*, a Japanese fleet destroyer that ran aground in 1944, include two large propeller shafts, parts of the turbine housing, gun barrels, fire extinguisher, a machine gun, plating and some shells next to a large chain. Also look for the remains of a Japanese ship dubbed the **George Bush Wreck**, which was supposedly sunk by the former U.S. president when he was a young WWII pilot.

The untamed stretches of Velasco Reef are home to silvertip sharks.

KEVIN DAVIDSON
"Herds" of bumphead parrotfish patrol the open reefs.

# Marine Life

Palau's marine life is greatly varied, with at least 900 fish species, 700 corals and myriad invertebrates. On the larger end of the marine creature scale, sperm whales, dolphin schools, whale sharks, dugongs and even orcas have been seen in Palau's waters. Macrophotography subjects like shrimps, mandarinfish and unusual nudibranchs are profuse. In between, a whole spectrum of marine animals can be found. The listing below represents just a sampling of the great range of life found in the Palau archipelago.

KEVIN DAVIDSON

Remember that common names are used freely but are notoriously inaccurate and inconsistent. The two-part scientific name, usually shown in italics, is more precise. It consists of a genus name followed by a species name. A genus is a group of closely related species that share common features. A species is a recognizable group within a genus whose members are capable of interbreeding. Where the species or genus is unknown, the naming reverts to the next known level: family (F), class (C) or phylum (Ph).

## Common Vertebrates

emperor angelfish (juvenile)
*Pomacanthus imperator*

regal angelfish
*Pygoplites diacanthus*

six-banded angelfish
*Pomacanthus sexstriatus*

bigeye jack
*Caranx sexfasciatus*

bluestripe snapper
*Lutjanus rufolineatus*

blue tang
*Paracanthurus hepatus*

blackfin soldierfish
*Myripristis adusta*

fire goby
*Nemateleotris magnifica*

saddled grouper
*Cephalopholis sexmaculata*

spinefin squirrelfish
*Sargocentron spiniferum*

spotted sweetlip
*Plectorhinchus chaetodontoides*

bignose unicornfish
*Naso vlamingii*

blunthead parrotfish
*Scarus microhinos*

longnose filefish
*Oxymonacanthus longirostris*

longnose hawkfish
*Oxycirrhites typus*

## Common Invertebrates

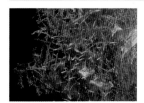

black coral
*Antipathes sp.*

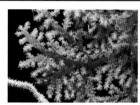

octocoral
*Siphonogorgia sp.*

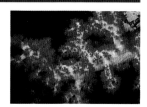

soft tree coral
*Dendronephthya sp.*

platter coral
*Acropora sp.*

bubble anemone
*Macrodactyla doreensis*

magnificent anemone
*Heteractis magnifica*

feather crinoid
*Comathina schlegleli*

sponge sea cucumber
*Synaptula sp.*

necklace sea star
*Fromia monilis*

bigeye shrimp
*Rhynchocinetes sp.*

whitecap shrimp
*Periclemenes sp.*

anemone crab
*Neopetrolisthes oshimai*

marine lake mussel
Cl. Pelycypoda

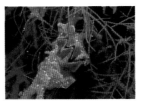

zigzag clam
*Hyotissa hyotis*

giant clam
*Tridacna gigas*

## Unusual Marine Life

crocodilefish
F. Platycephalidae

leaf fish
*Taenianotus triacanthus*

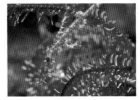

ornate ghost pipefish
*Solenostomus paradoxus*

chambered nautilus
*Nautilis pompilius*

spotted blenny
*Istiblennius sp.*

banded fantail pipefish
*Doryrhamphus dactyliophorus*

BOB HALSTEAD

# Hazardous Marine Life

Marine animals almost never attack divers, but many have defensive and offensive weaponry that can be triggered if they feel threatened or annoyed. The ability to recognize hazardous creatures is a valuable asset in avoiding accident and injury. The following are some of the potentially hazardous creatures most commonly found in Palau.

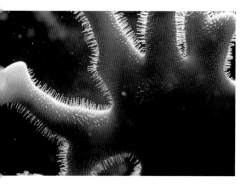

## Fire Coral

Although often mistaken for stony coral, fire coral is a hydroid colony that secretes a hard, calcareous skeleton. Fire coral grows in many different shapes, often encrusting or taking the form of a variety of reef structures. In Palau, look for it along the upper reefs near the drop-off. It is usually identifiable by its tan, mustard or brown color and finger-like columns with whitish tips. The entire colony is covered by tiny pores and fine, hair-like projections nearly invisible to the unaided eye. Fire coral "stings" by discharging small, specialized cells called nematocysts. Contact causes a burning sensation that lasts for several minutes and may produce red welts on the skin. Do not rub the area, as you will only spread the stinging particles. Cortisone cream can reduce the inflammation and antihistamine cream is good for killing the pain. Serious stings should be treated by a doctor.

## Jellyfish

The stings of a jelly are released by nematocysts contained in the trailing tentacles. The rule of thumb is the longer the tentacles, the more painful the sting. Keep an eye out for jellyfish with trailing tentacles, especially near the surface. In some

medusa jellyfish

KEVIN DAVIDSON

marine lakes in Palau, the jellies still sting, especially *Casiopea medusae*, which often appears upside-down on the seafloor, looking like a pulsing sea anemone.

On the outer reefs, man-o-war and sea wasps are found. Stings should be treated immediately with a decontaminant such as vinegar, rubbing alcohol, baking soda, papain, or dilute household ammonia. Beware that some people may have a stronger reaction than others, in which case you should prepare to resuscitate and seek medical aid.

## Cone Shell

Do not touch or pick up cone shells even though they are quite attractive. All cones are venomous, with *Conus geographus* being responsible for a number of human deaths. In Palau, you will see them almost exclusively at night and they prey on worms, other mollusks and fish.

The venom of a cone can be dangerous to humans even after the animal is dead, so it is best to not pick up any cone while diving. These mollusks deliver their venomous sting by shooting a tiny poison dart from their funnel-like proboscis. Stings will cause numbness and can be followed by muscular paralysis or even respiratory paralysis and heart failure. Immobilize the victim, apply a pressure bandage, be prepared to use CPR, and seek urgent medical aid.

## Sea Urchin

Sea urchins tend to live in shallow areas near shore and come out of their shelters at night. They vary in coloration and size, with spines ranging from short and blunt to long and needle-sharp. In Palau, you may find them on the shipwrecks, in the shallow "muck diving" areas and around large corals head.

The spines are the urchin's most dangerous weapon, easily able to penetrate neoprene wetsuits, booties and gloves. The long-spined *Diadema* species are most common, and appear to have one large eye. The spines break off easily and often break during extraction, so remove them very slowly and carefully. Stings can range from irritating to highly intense. Treat minor punctures by extracting any spines and immersing in nonscalding hot water. If a spine becomes imbedded, it will eventually work its way out. More serious injuries require medical attention.

## Sea Snake

Air-breathing reptiles with a venom that's 20 times stronger than any land snake, sea snakes release venom only when feeding or under extreme distress—so most defensive bites do not contain venom. Sea snakes rarely bite even if they are handled, but avoid touching them. To treat a sea snake bite, use a pressure bandage and immobilize the victim. Try to identify the snake, be prepared to administer CPR and seek urgent medical aid.

## Lionfish

Also known as turkeyfish or firefish, these slow, graceful fish extend their feathery pectoral fins as they swim. They have distinctive vertical brown or black bands alternating with narrower pink or white bands. Look for them around bait-fish schools on the black coral trees of Palau's shipwrecks. When threatened or provoked, lionfish may inject venom through dorsal spines that can penetrate booties, wetsuits and leather gloves. The wounds can be extremely painful. If stung, wash the wound and immerse in nonscalding hot water for 30 to 90 minutes. Administer pain medications if necessary.

## Scorpionfish & Stonefish

These well-camouflaged creatures are commonly seen on night dives and along the drop-offs in sandy and even silty bottoms. They are often difficult to spot since they typically rest quietly on the bottom or on coral, looking more like

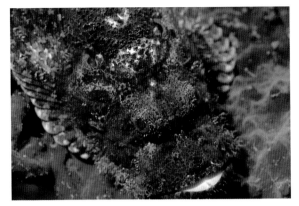
stonefish

rocks. But beware: they have poisonous spines along their dorsal fins, which can deliver an excruciating puncture wound. Practice good buoyancy control and watch where you put your hands. To treat a puncture, wash the wound and immerse in nonscalding hot water for 30 to 90 minutes to reduce spread of venom. These stings infect quickly so seek medical attention immediately.

## Barracuda

Barracuda are identifiable by their long, silver, cylindrical bodies and razor-like teeth protruding from an underslung jaw. They swim alone or in small groups, continually opening and closing their mouths, an action that looks daunting, but actually assists their respiration. In Palau, you'll often encounter large schools of blackbar and longnose barracuda. The solitary great barracuda will hover near divers to observe. While foreboding, they are really somewhat shy, though they may be attracted by shiny objects that resemble fishing lures. Irrigate a barracuda bite with fresh water and treat with antiseptics, anti-tetanus and antibiotics.

blackbar barracuda

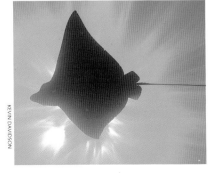
KEVIN DAVIDSON

eagle ray

## Ray

Identified by its diamond-shaped body and wide "wings," the ray can have anywhere from one to seven venomous spines at the base of its tail. Rays can be found in shallow waters and along the deeper reaches of the outer reefs. Many tend to rest on silty or sandy bottoms, often burying themselves in the sand.

Often only the eyes, gill slits and tail are visible. These creatures are harmless unless you sit or step on them. Though injuries are uncommon, wounds are always extremely painful, and often deep and infective. Immerse wound in non-scalding hot water and seek medical aid.

## Saltwater Crocodile

Palau is the only place in Micronesia where saltwater crocodiles are found. They live a mostly reclusive existence in remote Rock Island estuaries and in some inland fresh-water lakes. Encounters with divers are extremely rare, but if a large crocodile is reported in the area, opt to dive elsewhere. Juveniles appear occasionally, but Palau's crocs tend to be nocturnal, hanging out mostly near river mouths and mangroves. Treatment for bites is to stop any bleeding, reassure the patient, treat for shock and seek immediate medical treatment.

grey reef shark

## Shark

Sharks are encountered on virtually every dive in Palau, yet attacks on humans are rare and usually only occur in some misguided feeding attempt or to spearfishers. Avoid spearfishing, carrying fish baits or mimicking a wounded fish and your likelihood of being attacked will greatly diminish. In the event a shark does become aggressive, it is sometimes wise to rise to a shallower depth to get out of its territory. If it comes too close, stop and face the animal and watch it closely and quietly. Be prepared to push it away with a camera, knife or tank. If someone is bitten by a shark, stop the bleeding, reassure the patient, treat for shock and seek immediate medical aid.

# Diving Conservation & Awareness

Politics pervade much of the Pacific societies and Palau is a sterling example of this. One of the major political and economic ongoing debates is the issue of infrastructure development and its ill affects on environmental preservation. Threats to Palau's environment include plans to build a major highway spanning Babeldaob; an ambitious airport expansion; proposed golf courses; and hotel developments near mangrove and wetland areas. If not done properly, any of these projects has the potential to damage pristine areas. Heavy siltation, freshwater run-off and erosion from premature construction on the Babeldaob highway, for example, have already generated much concern about how the project will be fully implemented.

Government agencies oversee many of these projects and are aided by local, privately funded conservation groups. The Palau Conservation Society works to educate the public, promote responsible economic development and build support for environmental protection. Koror is home to the Micronesia Field Office branch of the Nature Conservancy. Specialists from the Convention on International Trade and Endangered Species (CITES) have come to research Palau. The Coral Reef Research Center hosts visiting biologists and publishes the results of their studies. Concerned village groups form family councils and state board environmental committees to ensure their land is not damaged.

But pressure from big business to develop more hotels, watersports and other tourist attractions threatens to take Palau in another direction. As Palau's

## Palau Conservation Areas

Palau has a number of conservation areas including the Ngemelis Islands, where fishing is prohibited within a mile of the islands. Seventy Islands Preserve (Ngerkewid Islands), Palau's first conservation area, is a turtle nesting area, where no fishing, hunting, camping or other environmental disturbance is. At Ngerumekaol (Ulong) Channel, fishing for groupers is regulated during spawning seasons.

Other sites overseen by traditional methods and regional boards include Ngeremeduu Bay, Ngardok Nature Preserve, Ngermai Conservation Area, Ngaraard Mangrove Conservation Area and the Ngaruangel Reserve north of Kayangel Atoll. The use of traditional taboos called "bul" are also imposed to conserve a specific regional resource. Some areas may be off limits to divers when this is in effect. This form of regulation is highly respected and is effective in preventing over-fishing and over-harvesting of resources.

popularity as a holiday destination continues to grow, so does the need for a supportable infrastructure.

The discussion of the environment and its protection is a cauldron of controversy that will boil in Palau for decades to come. As a visitor, you may find yourself in one of these debates when you mingle with the local folks. Economy minded Palauans point out that their kids can't eat fresh air and blue water and tourism is a major resource that should be developed. Ecologically minded Palauans acknowledge this economic fact of life, but say that development must be eco-friendly, well-planned, and properly studied and funded. If not, mass tourism and irresponsible growth could ruin the reason tourists come to Palau in the first place. Thankfully, most visitors tend to be very pro-environment, as diving and outdoor activities are the major reasons most people visit Palau.

Local children frolic on a pristine beach in Northern Palau.

# Responsible Diving

Dive sites tend to be located where the reefs and walls display the most beautiful corals and sponges. It only takes a moment—an inadvertently placed hand or knee, or a careless brush or kick with a fin—to destroy this fragile, living part of our delicate ecosystem. By following certain basic guidelines while diving, you can help preserve the ecology and beauty of the reefs:

1. Never drop boat anchors onto a coral reef and take care not to ground boats on coral. Encourage dive operators and regulatory bodies in their efforts to establish permanent moorings at appropriate dive sites.

2. Practice and maintain proper buoyancy control and avoid over-weighting. Be aware that buoyancy can change over the period of an extended trip. Initially you may breathe harder and need more weighting; a few days later you may breathe more easily and need less weight. Tip: Use your weight belt and tank position to maintain a horizontal position—raise them to elevate your feet, lower them to elevate your upper body. Also be careful about buoyancy loss: as you go deeper, your wetsuit compresses, as does the air in your BC.

3. Avoid touching living marine organisms with your body and equipment. Polyps can be damaged by even the gentlest contact. Never stand on or touch living coral. The use of gloves is no longer recommended: gloves make it too easy to hold on to the reef. The abrasion caused by gloves may be even more damaging to the reef than your hands are. If you must hold on to the reef, touch only exposed rock or dead coral.

4. Take great care in underwater caves. Spend as little time within them as possible, as your air bubbles can damage fragile organisms. Divers should take turns inspecting the interiors of small caves or under ledges to lessen the chances of damaging contact.

5. Be conscious of your fins. Even without contact, the surge from heavy fin strokes near the reef can do damage. Avoid full-leg kicks when diving close to the bottom and when leaving a photo scene. When you inadvertently kick something, stop kicking! It seems obvious, but some divers either panic or are totally oblivious when they bump something. When treading water in shallow reef areas, take care not to kick up clouds of sand. Settling sand can smother the delicate reef organisms.

6. Secure gauges, computer consoles and the octopus regulator so they're not dangling—they are like miniature wrecking balls to a reef.

7. When swimming in strong currents, be extra careful about leg kicks and handholds.

8. Photographers should take extra precautions as cameras and equipment affect buoyancy. Changing f-stops, framing a subject and maintaining position for a photo often conspire to prohibit the ideal "no-touch" approach on a reef. When you must use "holdfasts," choose them intelligently (i.e., use one finger only for leverage off an area of dead coral).

9. Resist the temptation to collect or buy coral or shells. Aside from the ecological damage, taking home marine souvenirs depletes the beauty of a site and spoils other divers' enjoyment.

10. Ensure that you take home all your trash and any litter you may find as well. Plastics in particular pose a serious threat to marine life.

11. Resist the temptation to feed fish. You may disturb their normal eating habits, encourage aggressive behavior or feed them food that is detrimental to their health.

12. Minimize your disturbance of marine animals. Don't ride on the backs of turtles or manta rays as this can cause them great anxiety.

8. Photographers should take extra precautions, as cameras and equipment affect buoyancy. Changing f-stops, framing a subject and maintaining position for a photo often conspire to prohibit the ideal "no-touch" approach on a reef. When you must use "holdfasts," choose them intelligently (i.e., use one finger only for leverage off an area of dead coral).

9. Resist the temptation to collect or buy coral or shells. Aside from the ecological damage, taking home marine souvenirs depletes the beauty of a site and spoils other divers' enjoyment.

10. Ensure that you take home all your trash and any litter you may find as well. Plastics in particular pose a serious threat to marine life.

11. Resist the temptation to feed fish. You may disturb their normal eating habits, encourage aggressive behavior or feed them food that is detrimental to their health.

12. Minimize your disturbance of marine animals. Don't ride on the backs of turtles or manta rays, as this can cause them great anxiety.

## Marine Conservation Organizations

The following groups are actively involved in promoting responsible diving practices, publicizing environmental marine threats, and lobbying for better policies.

### Local Organizations

**Palau Conservation Society**
P.O. Box 1811
Koror, Palau 96940
☎ 680-488-3993  fax: 680-488-3990
pcs@palaunet.com

**The Nature Conservancy
(Micronesia Field Office)**
P.O. Box 1738
Koror, Palau 96940
☎ 680-488-2017  fax: 680-488-4550

**The Coral Reef Research Center**
P.O. Box 1765
Koror, Palau 96940
☎ 680-488-5255  fax: 680-488-5513

### International Organizations

**CORAL: The Coral Reef Alliance**
☎ 510-848-0110
www.coral.org

**Project AWARE Foundation**
☎ 714-540-0251
www.projectaware.org

**Coral Forest**
☎ 415-788-REEF
www.blacktop.com/coralforest

**ReefKeeper International**
☎ 305-358-4600
www.reefkeeper.org

**Cousteau Society**
☎ 757-523-9335
www.cousteausociety.org

# Listings

## Telephone Calls

To call Palau, dial the international access code for the country you are calling from (from the U.S. it's 011) + 680 (Palau's country code) + the 7-digit local number.

## Accommodations

There are hotels for every budget and desire. You can stay at first class, every-amenity hotels right in town, or make arrangements to stay in local homes (homestays) or rustic resorts on far off islands. The Palau Pacific Resort and the Carp Island Resort are currently the only dedicated dive resorts in Palau, though the West Plaza chain's Coral Reef and By The Sea facilities are often used by divers. Most hotels and motels also work with the dive shops to make diving or snorkeling arrangements for guests.

### Tourist Office

Palau Visitors Authority
P.O. Box 256
Koror, Palau 96940
pva@palaunet.com
www.visit-palau.com
☎ 488-2793/1930
fax: 488-1453/1725

### Resorts

**Carp Island Resort**
(25 rooms)
P.O. Box 5
Koror, Palau 96940
☎ 488-2978  fax: 488-3155
carpcorp@palaunet.com
Seaside cottages, independent houses and suites. Home to the Palau Diving Center.

**Palau Pacific Resort**
(160 rooms)
P.O. Box 308
Koror, Palau 96940
☎ 488-2600  fax: 488-1601
ppr@palaunet.com
Deluxe guest rooms have garden views or ocean fronts. Home to Splash Diving Center.

**The Carolines Resort**
(7 rooms)
P.O. Box 399
Koror, Palau 96940

☎ 488-3754  fax: 488-3756
carolines@palaunet.com
Private bungalows overlooking the Rock Islands.

**Storyboard Beach Resort**
(6 rooms)
Peleliu State, Palau 96940
☎ 345-1019  fax: 345-1058
pdivers@palaunet.com
Private deluxe bungalows on the beach.

**Ngaraard Traditional Resort**
(3-room cottages)
P.O. Box 773
Koror, Palau 96940
☎ 488-1788  fax: 488-1725
ntr@palaunet.com
Thatched private beach cottages with view of the sunrise over reef.

# Hotels

**Airai View Hotel**
(91 rooms)
P.O. Box 37
Koror, Palau 96940
☎ 488-3530  fax: 488-3533
airaiview@palaunet.com

**Cocoro Hotel**
(48 rooms)
P.O. Box 1711
Koror, Palau 96940
☎ 488-5852  fax: 488-5855
maco@palaunet.com

**Hotel Nikko Palau**
(51 rooms)
P.O. Box 310
Koror, Palau 96940
☎ 488-2486  fax: 488-2878

**Malakal Central Hotel**
(18 rooms)
P. O. Box 6016
Koror, Palau 96940
☎ 488-1117  fax: 488-1075

**Outrigger Palasia Hotel**
(165 rooms)
P.O. Box 1256
Koror, Palau 96940
☎ 488-8888  fax: 488-8898
outrigger@palaunet.com

**Palau Hotel**
(35 rooms)
P.O. Box 457
Koror, Palau 96940
☎ 488-1703  fax: 488-1317

**Palau Marina Hotel**
(20 rooms)
P.O. Box 142
Koror, Palau 96940
☎ 488-1786  fax: 488-1070
marina@palaunet.com

**The Penthouse Hotel**
(12 rooms)
P.O. Box 6013
Koror, Palau 96940
☎ fax: 488-1942
the-penthouse@palaunet.com

**Sunrise Villa Hotel**
(21 rooms)
P.O. Box 6009
Koror, Palau 96940
☎ 488-4590  fax: 488-4593
sunrise@palaunet.com

**VIP Guest Hotel**
(22 rooms)
P.O. Box 18
Koror, Palau 96940
☎ 488-1502  fax: 488-1429

**Waterfront Villa**
(22 rooms)
P.O. Box 1036
Koror, Palau 96940
☎/fax: 488-2904
waterfront.villa@palaunet.com

**West Plaza Coral Reef Hotel**
(14 rooms)
P.O. Box 280
Koror, Palau 96940
☎ 488-5355  Fax: 488-1783
west.plaza@palaunet.com

**West Plaza Desekel Hotel**
(30 rooms)
P.O. Box 280
Koror, Palau 96940
☎ 488-2521  fax: 488-2136
west.plaza@palaunet.com

**West Plaza Downtown Hotel**
(22 rooms)
P.O. Box 280
Koror, Palau 96940
☎ 488-1671  fax: 488-1783
west.plaza@palaunet.com

**West Plaza Hotel, By the Sea**
(34 rooms)
P.O. Box 280
Koror, Palau 96940
☎ 488-2133  fax: 488-2136
west.plaza@palaunet.com

**West Plaza Hotel, Malakal**
(27 rooms)
P.O. Box 280
Koror, Palau 96940
☎ 488-5290  fax: 488-2136
west.plaza@palaunet.com

# Motels

### King's Motel
(13 rooms)
P.O. Box 424
Koror, Palau 96940
☎ 488-2964  fax: 488-3273
king'sent@palaunet.com

### D.W. Motel
(14 rooms)
P.O. Box 738
Koror, Palau 96940
☎ 488-2641  fax: 488-1725

### H.K. Motel
(9 rooms)
P.O. Box 61
Koror, Palau 96940
☎ 488-2764  fax: 488-4609

### Lehns Motel & Apartments
(22 rooms)
P.O. Box 653
Koror, Palau 96940
☎/fax: 488-1486
lehns.motel@palaunet.com

### Tree-D Motel & Apartments
(24 rooms)
P.O. Box 1703
Koror, Palau 96940
☎ 488-3856  fax: 488-4584

### Yuhi Motel
(13 rooms)
P.O. Box 766
Koror, Palau 96940
☎ 488-5955  fax: 488-5959
yuhi@palaunet.com

# Homestays

### Reiko's Inn
(5 rooms)
Peleliu State, Palau 96940
☎ 345-1106

### Wenty's Sunset Inn
(4 rooms)
Peleliu State, Palau 96940
☎ 345-1080
Quiet, beach atmosphere, collection of
WWII relics on the premises.

### Beach Front Homes (Melekeok State)
(8 rooms)
P.O. Box 6042
Koror, Palau 96940
☎ 654-1001  fax: 654-1003
Peaceful beachfront property near
amenities.

### NTA Guest Houses (Ngardmau State)
P.O. Box 445
Koror, Palau 96940
☎ 488-2683  fax: 488-2800
Furnished two-bedroom houses with
fully equipped kitchen. Near amenities
and cultural sites.

### Maria's Homestay (Ngchesar State)
P.O. Box 6025
Koror, Palau 96940

☎ 622-1086
Single room, features quiet and relax-
ing atmosphere, historical
and cultural sites within walking distance.

### Patrick's Homestay (Ngchesar State)
P.O. Box 1067
Koror, Palau 96940
☎ 622-1067
Single room, features quiet and relax-
ing atmosphere, historical
and cultural sites within walking distance.

### Sisca's Homestay (Ngchesar State)
P.O. Box 6025
Koror, Palau 96940
☎ 622-1060
Single room, features quiet and relax-
ing atmosphere, historical and cultural
sites within walking distance.

### Yada's Homestay (Ngchesar State)
P.O. Box 6025
Koror, Palau 96940
☎ 622-1067
Single room, features quiet and relax-
ing atmosphere, historical and cultural
sites within walking distance.

# Diving Services

### Antelope
P.O. Box 1722
Koror, Palau 96940
antelope@palaunet.com
☎ 488-1059  fax: 488-2077
**Dive Shop**: no  **Rentals**: yes
**Air**: yes
**Courses**: PADI Open Water to
Divemaster, some specialties
**Boats**: three dive boats
**Trips**: Daily trips to popular dive sites;
charters; fishing; sightseeing tours

### Aqua Magic
P.O. Box 37
Koror, Palau 96940
aquamagic@palaunet.com
www.aquamagicpalau.com
☎ 488-1119  fax: 488-5663
**Dive Shop**: no  **Rentals**: yes
**Air**: yes
**Courses**: PADI Open Water to
Divemaster
**Boats**: three twin-engine open dive
boats
**Trips**: Daily trips to popular dive sites

### Dive Palau
P.O. Box 1904
Koror, Palau 96940
keithpda@palaunet.com
www.palaudive.com
☎/fax: 488-3548
**Dive Shop**: no  **Rentals**: yes
**Air**: yes
**Courses**: PADI Open Water to
Divemaster, specialties
**Boats**: 30ft cabin dive boat
**Trips**: Daily two- or three-tank trips to
popular dive sites; night dives available
on request

### Fish N' Fins (Palau Marina Hotel)
P.O. Box 142
Koror, Palau 96940
fishnfin@palaunet.com
www.fishnfins.com
☎ 488-2637  fax: 488-1070
**Dive Shop**: yes  **Rentals**: yes
**Air**: yes, nitrox available

**Courses**: PADI Open Water to
Assistant Instructor and all specialties;
IANTD Nitrox, Advanced Nitrox and
Instructor
**Boats**: Three 29ft cabin dive boats with
twin engines.
**Trips**: Daily two- or three-tank trips to
popular dive sites; night dives; trips to
Jellyfish Lake

### Island Nation
P.O. Box 1714-W108
Koror, Palau 96940
islandnation@palaunet.com
www.eco-island.com
☎ 488-5322  fax: 488-5410
**Dive Shop**: no  **Rentals**: no
**Air**: yes
**Courses**: no
**Boats**: 24ft Bayliner Trophy
**Trips**: Daily two- or three-tank trips to
popular dive sites; night dives; camping
in the Rock Islands; Babeldoab eco-
tours; kayaking; fishing

### NECO Marine
P.O. Box 129
Koror, Palau 96940
necomarine@palaunet.com
www.seapalau.com
☎ 488-1755  fax: 488-3014
Toll-free: 1-800-348-0842
**Dive Shop**: yes  **Rentals**: yes
**Air**: yes, nitrox available
**Courses**: PADI courses available in
Japanese, English and German
**Boats**: Seven 33ft covered dive boats
w/freshwater showers and dry storage
**Trips**: Day diving trips to all sites; two-
or three-tank trips; night dives; fishing;
snorkeling, sightseeing

### Palau Diving Center (Carp Island Resort)
P.O. Box 5
Koror, Palau 96940
carpcorp@palaunet.com
☎ 488-2978  fax: 488-3155
**Dive Shop**: yes  **Rentals**: yes
**Air**: yes

**Courses**: PADI, JP and Naui Open Water to Advanced
**Boats**: Two 29ft Yamahas with 200hp and 150hp outboards
**Trips**: Daily two- or three-tank trips to popular dive sites; night dives; fishing, kayaking

### Paradise Divers, Ltd.
P.O. Box 1287
Koror, Palau 96940
paradisedivers@palaunet.com
☎/fax: 488-5008
**Dive Shop**: no  **Rentals**: yes
**Air**: yes
**Courses**: PADI Open Water to Divemaster
**Boats**: 50ft fiberglass with twin 375ft outboards; 29ft fiberglass with 170ft outboard
**Trips**: Daily trips to popular dive sites

### Peleliu Divers (Storyboard Beach Resort)
P.O. Box 8071
Koror, Palau 96940
pdivers@palaunet.com
www.plaza16.mbn.or.jp/~palau/pdivers.htm
☎/fax: 345-1058
**Dive Shop**: no  **Rentals**: yes
**Air**: yes
**Courses**: no
**Boats**: 29ft twin-engine dive boat
**Trips**: Daily trips to Southern Palau

### Sam's Dive Tours/Planet Blue Kayak Tours
P.O. Box 7076
Koror, Palau 96940
samstour@palaunet.com
www.samstour.com
☎ 488-1062  fax: 488-5003
Toll-free: 800-794-9767
**Dive Shop**: yes  **Rentals**: yes
**Air**: yes, nitrox available

**Courses**: PADI Open Water to Instructor
**Boats**: Eight twin-engine dive and fishing boats
**Trips**: Daily two- or three-tank trips to popular and secret dive sites; night dives; special trips to Kayangel Atoll and Angaur; catch and release sportfishing; sail charters; kayaking and land tours

### Southern Marine Divers
P.O. Box 1598
Koror, Palau 96940
smd@palaunet.com
☎ 488-2345  fax: 488-3128
**Dive Shop**: yes  **Rentals**: yes
**Air**: yes
**Courses**: PADI Open Water, some specialties
**Boats**: three twin-engine open dive boats
**Trips**: Daily trips to popular dive sites

### Splash Diving Center (Palau Pacific Resort)
P.O. Box 847
Koror, Palau 96940
splash@palaunet.com
www.divepalau.com
☎ 488-2600  fax: 488-1741
**Dive Shop**: yes  **Rentals**: yes
**Air**: yes
**Courses**: PADI and resort courses, refresher courses and open-water referrals
**Boats**: Four dive boats, various sizes
**Trips**: Daily two-tank trips to popular dive sites; charters; trips to Jellyfish Lake

### UBDI Blue Marlin
P.O. Box 669
Koror, Palau 96940
bclau.tour@palaunet.com
☎/fax: 488-2214

# Live-Aboards

**Lesson II** *Palau Sport*
P.O. Box 1455
Koror, Palau 96940
☎ 488-1120  fax: 488-1125
palausport@palaunet.com
**Home Port**: Malakal
**Description**: 126ft mothership and three tenders
**Accommodations**: eight two-bed rooms, three four-bed rooms
**Trips:** mothership stays out (near Ngemelis) for 3-4 weeks, dive tenders transfer guests to port and dive sites
**Passenger Capacity**: 28
**Other**: book through Sport Tours in Tokyo, Japan (☎ 81-3-3856-0130); onboard compressor; E6 processing; fully air conditioned

**Ocean Hunter** *Palau*
P.O. Box 964
Koror, Palau 96940
☎ 488-2637/5416  fax: 488-5418
ocean.hunter@palaunet.com
www.oceanhunter.com
**Home Port**: Koror
**Description**: 60ft steel luxury dive boat; 15ft inflatable and 21ft fiberglass tenders
**Accommodations**: three air-conditioned cabins
**Trips**: 7 to 14 days of unlimited diving
**Passenger Capacity**: 6
**Other**: gourmet food; PADI courses from Open Water to Assistant Instructor, specialties include nitrox, wreck diving and deep dives; IANTD basic to advanced nitrox; guaranteed unlimited diving

*Palau Aggressor II*
P.O. Box 1714-P106
Koror, Palau 96940
☎/fax: 488-6075
paggressor@palaunet.com
www.pac-aggressor.com
**Home Port**: Koror
**Description**: 105ft luxury live-aboard
**Accommodations**: eight staterooms with queen, double or single berths, private ensuite baths
**Trips**: 7 days, with 5½ days of diving
**Passenger Capacity**: 16
**Other**: fully air-conditioned; daily E6 processing, light tables, large photo set-up tables on dive deck; PADI and NAUI certification and specialty courses; nitrox air and training; rebreather training; unlimited air; hot tub; nightly entertainment includes films and slide shows; airport transfers

**Peter Hughes** *Sun Dancer II*
Street address: P.O Box 487
Koror, Palau 96940
☎/fax: 488-3983
dancer@palaunet.com
peterhughes.com
**Home Port**: Koror
**Description**: 138ft aluminum mono hull; two (32 and 28ft) tenders with 400hp jet engines
**Accommodations**: 10 staterooms
**Trips**: 7 and 10 night itineraries, up to fours dives/day
**Passenger Capacity**: 20
**Other**: two on-board compressors; air-conditioning; E6 processing, photo and video instruction, camera rentals; gear rental; Open Water, Advanced and specialty certification available.

# Index

dive sites covered in this book appear in **bold** type

# Lonely Planet Pisces Books

The **Diving & Snorkeling** guides cover top destinations worldwide. Beautifully illustrated with full-color photos throughout, the series explores the best diving and snorkeling areas and prepares divers for what to expect when they get there. Each site is described in detail, with information on suggested ability levels, depth, visibility and, of course, marine life. There's basic topside information as well for each destination.

## Also check out dive guides to:

Australia: Southeast Coast

Bahamas: Family Islands
& Grand Bahama

Bahamas: Nassau
& New Providence

Bali & the Komodo Region

Bermuda

Bonaire

British Virgin Islands

Cocos Island

Curaçao

Dominica

Florida Keys

Jamaica

Monterey Peninsula &
Northern California

Pacific Northwest

Puerto Rico

Red Sea

Roatan & Honduras'
Bay Islands

Scotland

Seychelles

Southern California

St. Maarten, Saba,
& St. Eustatius

Texas

Turks & Caicos

U.S. Virgin Islands

Vanuatu

# Lonely Planet

| | |
|---|---|
| **travel guidebooks** | in-depth coverage with background and recommendations |
| **shoestring guides** | for those with plenty of time and limited money |
| **condensed guides** | highlights the best a destination has to offer |
| **citySync** | digital city guides for Palm™ OS |
| **outdoor guides** | walking, cycling, diving and watching wildlife series |
| **phrasebooks** | including unusual languages and two-way dictionaries |
| **city maps and road atlases** | essential navigation tools |
| **world food** | explores local cuisine and produce |
| **out to eat** | a city's best places to eat and drink |
| **read this first** | invaluable pre-departure guides |
| **healthy travel** | practical advice for staying well on the road |
| **journeys** | great reading for armchair explorers |
| **pictorial** | lavishly illustrated coffee table books |
| **ekno** | low-cost phonecard with e-services |
| **TV series and videos** | stories from on the road |
| **website** | for chat, upgrades, and up-to-date destination facts |
| **lonely planet images** | online photo library |

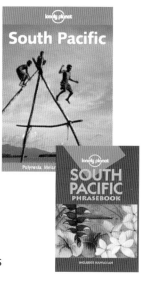

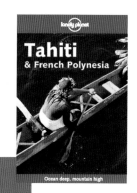

## Download free guidebook upgrades at:
### *www.lonelyplanet.com*

# Lonely Planet Online

## Get the latest travel information before you leave or while you're on the road

**Lonely Planet online.** Lonely Planet's award-winning website has insider information on hundreds of destinations from Amsterdam to Zimbabwe complete with interactive maps and relevant links. The site also offers the latest travel news, recent reports from travellers on the road, guidebook upgrades, a travel links site, an online book buying option and a lively traveller's bulletin board.

**Planet Talk** is the quarterly print newsletter full of gossip, advice, anecdotes and author articles. It provides an antidote to the being-at-home blues and lets you plan and dream for the next trip. Contact the nearest Lonely Planet office for your free copy.

**Comet**, the free Lonely Planet newsletter, comes via email once a month. It's loaded with travel news, advice, dispatches from authors, travel competitions and letters from readers. To subscribe, click on the Comet subscription link on the front page of the website.

### www.lonelyplanet.com or AOL keyword: lp

# Lonely Planet Publications

**Australia**
P.O. Box 617, Hawthorn, Victoria 3122
☎ (03) 9819 1877  fax: (03) 9819 6459
email: talk2us@lonelyplanet.com.au

**USA**
150 Linden Street
Oakland, California 94607
☎ (510) 893 8555, (800) 275 8555
fax: (510) 893 8563
email: info@lonelyplanet.com

**UK**
10a Spring Place,
London NW5 3BH
☎ (0171) 428 4800 fax: (0171) 428 4828
email: go@lonelyplanet.co.uk

**France**
1 rue du Dahomey
75011 Paris
☎ 01 55 25 33 00 fax: 01 55 25 33 01
email: bip@lonelyplanet.fr

**www.lonelyplanet.com**